PEOPLE AND WORK

Human and industrial relations in library and information work

PEOPLE AND WORK

Human and industrial relations in library and information work

Edited and compiled by
Rosemary Raddon

Head of Department of Information and Library Management at Newcastle upon Tyne Polytechnic

LIBRARY ASSOCIATION PUBLISHING
LONDON
A CLIVE BINGLEY BOOK

© Rosemary Raddon for the compilation 1991
the contributors for the articles 1991

Published by
Library Association Publishing Ltd
7 Ridgmount Street
London WC1E 7AE

All rights reserved. No part of this publication may be photocopied, recorded or otherwise reproduced, stored in a retrieval system or transmitted in any form or by any electronic or mechanical means without the prior permission of the copyright owner and publisher.

First published 1991

British Library Cataloguing in Publication Data

People and work : human and industrial relations in library and information work.
  1. Libraries. Personnel management
  I. Raddon, Rosemary
  023

ISBN 0-85157-431-9

Typeset in 10/12pt Palacio by Library Association Publishing Ltd
Printed and made in Great Britain by Billing and Sons Ltd, Worcester

Contents

Contributors	viii
Preface	ix
Introduction	xi

Part One The working environment: contexts and issues — 1
Introduction to Part One — 1
1 Race — 3
2 Gender — 7
3 Harmonization — 13
4 Performance indicators and performance-related pay — 16
5 Conditions of work and the negotiating machinery — 24
6 The negotiating process — 31
7 Counselling support — 39
8 Psychodynamic aspects of industrial relations
    Rossana Kendall — 43

Part Two Perspectives: viewpoints from practitioners, professionals and unions — 53
Introduction to Part Two — 53
9 The role of the Library Association *David Ruse* — 55
10 Industrial relations: a NALGO perspective
    John Findlay — 63
11 The NATFHE perspective *David Triesman* — 71
12 The GMB perspective *John Edmonds* — 84
13 Introduction to viewpoints of practitioners — 89
14 Viewpoints of practitioners — 91
    1: *London Borough of Wandsworth*
    Interviews with Lance Garrett and John Hall — 91
    2: *Politics and practitioners*
    Interview with a Director of Housing — 98

v

Part Three Implications for managers: Information
            sources   109
Introduction to Part Three   109
15 Implications for managers   111
    1: coping with change   111
    2: the political aspects of change   116
16 Abbreviations and glossary   123
17 Bibliography   126
18 Journals   142
19 Organizations   144
20 Training resources   151
21 Legislation   152

Index   163

For my Father

Contributors

John Edmonds General Secretary, GMB
John Findlay Assistant National Officer, NALGO
Lance Garrett Director of Leisure and Amenity Services, London Borough of Wandsworth
John Hall Staff-Side Secretary (NALGO), London Borough of Wandsworth
Rossana Kendall Training Officer, London Borough of Barking and Dagenham
Rosemary Raddon Head of Department of Information and Library Management, Newcastle Polytechnic
David Ruse Head of Policy and Development, Berkshire County Library and Information Service (formerly Assistant Director, Employment and Resources, Library Association)
David Triesman DES Negotiating Secretary, NATFHE

Preface

Rosemary Raddon

People at work, or employer/employee relationships, need to be seen within the current climate of widely differing ideologies and philosophies – political, cultural, economic, technical and social. Responses in the workplace to these issues range through simplistic opposition, political manipulation, grudging acceptance, acceptance by default and wholehearted responsiveness. Such responses are a result of factors as diverse as political beliefs, socio-economic factors, changes in legislation or privatization policies and practices.

In the context of library and information services such issues and changes affect and determine service delivery, and in the process employer/employee relationships change. Such changes have to be managed, and the tensions and dynamics understood. All have implications for the profession, career patterns and workplace relationships.

Personal and organizational relationships relate not only to these 'external' factors, but also to changing boundaries and changing sub-groups of the 'internal' organization. The external world affects the stability and dynamics of systems. Inter-group, intra-group and personal relationships then all shift. The introduction of market-led economies, for example, from the external world, may cause technical sub-systems to change in relation to other sub-systems, as the techniques of cost recovery become increasingly important. The balance and internal structure of the organization can then alter as a result. Management responses then need to be identified and implemented.

It is important that these issues are supported through appropriate curriculum development and continuing education opportunities in the library schools. In turn such programmes must be linked to employer needs and demands, and to training policies and practices in the public and private sectors. These in turn are affected by resources, causing the mechanisms of training and development to change. As services alter and as these developments are supported through education and training, the perceptions of the users and potential professionals also change. They in turn affect organizations and their internal dynamics, as new perceptions and ideas are integrated into existing systems. Continuing professional development must underpin change.

Within this context, this book is intended to provide a background and practical advice for those in middle management. It is aimed at those at mid career level who are involved in managing people in the workplace, mainly in the public sector. The contents are culled from a wide range of experiences and all the contributors write with a knowledge of the context. No particular aspect of the employer/employee relationship is pursued in great depth, such as legislation, as this is not a legal textbook, but information sources and references to specialist advice and agencies are given.

The book falls naturally into three parts. As people at work are all affected by the rapidly changing social, political and economic issues, an overview of some of these major changes is given, again with particular reference to the public sector. Some of the most pertinent issues affecting the workplace, and particularly in the library and information profession, are considered. These include areas such as race, gender and performance-related pay. Change is also effected through the negotiating machinery, and managers and workers need the skills of counselling and negotiating both to use the machinery and to support organizational change. Managers also need to be aware of some of the psychological aspects of an organization, and so some psychodynamic theories are included, as these underpin relationships between managers and managed, and between organizations and external forces.

The second part flows from this overview, and illustrates how many of these issues are managed in practical situations and how they surface in all areas of industrial relations. So current thinking and practices are reflected by the collection of perspectives from some major unions and from the Library Association. Industrial relations issues in relation to change are also reflected in the interviews, which clearly show the reaction and response to change from two differing political viewpoints.

The third part illustrates some of the managerial implications of change. It also provides information and guidance to sources of information, including abbreviations in common usage, book and journal resources, organizations, training resources, and an outline of some of the major pieces of legislation affecting the workplace. All these are referred to implicitly or explicitly in earlier chapters.

So the general theories set the scene, perspectives and case studies illustrate responses, and managerial issues and further information provide support. Manager's notes are given at the end of each section, and are intended as a practical guide to support the text. Each part stands alone for ease of reference, but all are inter-related.

Introduction

Management context – the changing scene
Management is usually perceived as the focus and agent of change, and the individual employee is a crucial element in this process. The ways in which management has responded to change in relation to differing political and social concepts are varied. Techniques, theories and ideas are constantly being reconsidered in response to the next shift in concepts or movements. Industrial and employee relations are also constantly altering and so illustrate perfectly one area of change where management ideology, techniques and personal and organizational relationships can focus and grow. Issues such as general government policies, rapid technological developments, social concerns, variations in power and authority, all contribute to this focus on change. Images, as in other walks of life, are crucial, and management, employee and union images are changing fast in the current climate. The supporting web of training, development and careers work, counselling and psycho-analytical support contributes to this mosaic. At the centre of all these stimuli should be a concern for the individual, providing the core of the changing conceptualization of employee relationships.

The current general context of employer/employee relationships is that of a capitalist economy, functioning alongside and with some left-wing ideologies and practices, while the rhetoric of both hides their essential differences and similarities. Detailed analyses attached to these labels are not the purpose of this book, but the tensions caused contribute to the subject. The tensions are caused partly by this cloud of rhetoric, so that analysis is difficult and protracted, and partly by ideological differences, including left-wing dilemmas opposed by right-wing certainties. At the same time both power groupings are unwilling or unable to admit that they have some areas in common. In addition the moral debate has been obscured and confused, so that the ideologies of the current majority party have tended to concentrate on pragmatic and identifiable elements in social change, such as trade unionism and industrial relations.

Such focusing has tended to act as a smokescreen to obscure the real politics of the governing party and so the root of the real tensions. This area is where the analysis has to take place at the highest political level. From such 'core' political ideas stems the ideological legislation and current concern with a range of market forces, economic and social theories, the power of the state, destabilizing of local control and change in educational control. All contribute to the present employer/employee situation and are clear indications of in-depth, as against superficial, political motives and strategies.

Demographic shifts, economic problems, the decline of traditional heavy industries with a strong union power base, the North–South divide, the end of consensus, high economic and individualistic material expectations in some sectors of the population, a widening class gap, structural unemployment and the gradual ending of the post-war concept of a 'caring' economy are also contributory factors. Others include the applications of new technology, and changes in emphasis in the declining and reorganized public sector. Increasing centralization, changes in curriculum control, general 'central' control, the decline in belief in the state as a benevolent force, and in the belief that unions have a strong role to play in linking productivity with care for workers, play their parts. Shrinking local authority control is also a factor. Rises in home-ownership numbers and of those in self-employment, and a marked shift to the service and white collar industries are also important. Employment changes in terms of legislation, the Single European Market, a declining union membership, health and safety legislation and equal pay concerns, plus issues of race and gender are all familiar developments. Change in the ethos of local authorities, including a greater degree of 'politicization', with shifts in the role of senior officers, greater participation in the political arena of women, black people and blue-collar workers, have all added to the impetus of change. There are also many tensions in local authorities between those committed to the public service ethos and those who, while committed to it, use services as a weapon against political policies with which they violently disagree. Social concerns are also being voiced, as an apparent decrease in concern for the 'have nots' becomes more evident in some quarters.

The concept of local accountability is creating tensions between those labelled 'professionals' and those labelled 'politicians'. These tensions in turn cause uncertainties and shifts in the workplace and in workplace relationships. An example is the prevalence of market forces contributing to change, through the need to provide an efficient and effective bureaucracy which is also highly motivated.

This implies that politicians and professionals in the public sector have to work more closely together, and so the roles of both become blurred, making organizations more sensitized to demand. Recent changes in some county library restructuring are an example of this. The role of the unions then becomes confused between concern for union members, protection of jobs in the market-led and privatization economy, and a neglect of the consumers, creating further tensions between central and local policies. There is a blurring of previously clearly defined boundaries and power bases.

Current legislation is also increasing the tensions between local and national government, with confusing messages of central control, countered by the need for strong local accountability and independence, and more involvement by the consumers of services. Legislation has also undermined the traditional union stance of collective action and collective bargaining. The Local Government and Housing Act (1989) is a major piece of legislation which restricts political activity. It also makes sweeping reforms in the areas of capital expenditure by local councils and the use of income from council housing as subsidies for other services. However, the political scene is changing so rapidly in the early 1990s that sharp divisions between broad left and broad right can no longer be applied in a simplistic manner to changes in both ethos and legislation.

Changes in traditional class structures and patterns of loyalty can also be seen. In some of the newer plants and in technology-based industries, membership of unions is either declining or, in some areas, shifting to single-union situations and 'no strike' deals. This shift also illustrates further ideological dilemmas for unions and reflects rapidly changing situations in the context of politically controlled economic and social developments. Recent legislation for further control on industrial action and the abolition of the pre-entry closed shop illustrates radical political change to curb unions.

Although at present great changes are taking place, there are opposing and supporting forces for trade unionism. Some 'strong' managements welcome union organization as one effective way of communicating with the workforce, and are aware that without this restraining and balancing force the dynamics of an organization can be disrupted. Many of the so-called 'alternatives', such as councils, committees and cooperatives, have tended to founder as an essential dynamic is missing. Group dynamics and group theories are relevant to these issues, but balance with and among workers is essential if organizations are to flourish without resorting to damaging legislation.

In this arena of industrial relations, the old knee-jerk reactions are no longer effective and there are changes in patterns of thinking and behaviour. Unions are concerned with the development of new policies, strategies and services. Such changes have an impact on organizations and organizational climates. They may also produce difficulties, caused sometimes by the so-called 'new realists' and sometimes by the so-called 'traditionalists'. However, concentration on strategies and services alone is often felt to be insufficient, and employee relations must also be considered in relation to the quality of working life. One of the ironies of this situation is that consideration of this issue brings together some of the elements of both right- and left-wing ideologies. A concern with quality could, in many ways, help alleviate some of the tensions caused by the external forces of change already identified.

A fundamental concern with the wider political climate has marked an important change for both employers and unions. Legislative changes may well have caused union members to reconsider their relationships with the parent body and with the union, so that an individual concern with the process of union membership may be emerging. The balance between individual freedom and union responsibility will doubtless continue to be debated, as the ideologies represented grow further apart. A recent ACAS *Annual report* (1989), highlights the gap between unions and management, linked to declining membership. This is a particularly strong trend in the private sector. This trend has in turn highlighted the issue of non-unionism, which will become crucial as the public sector declines. Worker mobility and high material expectations are two factors which add impetus, in an economy with rapidly changing patterns of work.

Ideologies are also contributing to change at a 'hidden' level, and particularly where 'hard left', or indeed 'hard right', infiltration into unions is altering the balance of power. This is an area which is difficult to quantify, but such movements do exist and are having effects on industrial relations.

The current government emphasizes its belief in the need for individual choice, through mechanisms such as balloting for industrial action and the re-election of union leaders, to protect individuals who do not want to participate in industrial action. The opposite ideology is that workers must be protected in an increasingly competitive and exploitative work situation. They should also share in and participate in the benefits of their work. Single-union and 'no strike' agreements form part of this picture, and have in some cases sharpened divisions. An example which highlighted the dilemmas was the recent single-union dispute with Ford of America at Dundee. This lost local jobs as the unions finally pulled out of

Introduction

the agreement. These strategic and ideological dilemmas affect both individual unions and the TUC. The legislation also reflects the changing tension between Government and Opposition.

Both approaches have to be seen in this current context of rapid change and particularly in the breaking up of previously neat and tidy divisions and labels. These have applied to class, politics and occupation for example, but with such fast changes in a market economy, mirrored by political power shifts and the alteration to traditional political power bases, many such labels are no longer valid. In many cases the power of the unions has declined within the overall context, and so they are no longer able to 'deliver the goods', leading to falling membership and a further twist in the declining spiral. The TUC conference of 1990 illustrated these points and dilemmas well, when both politicians and union leaders tried to balance ideological, legal, social and economic demands and practicalities.

The changing role of the TUC is part of this dilemma. It now represents a concern with workers and the politics of the workplace in a society that is shifting towards a different perspective. The TUC originally was an effective bureaucracy whose main objective was that of putting pressure on the government of the day, through its own structure and through the civil service, to protect its members – the workers. This machinery and organization are now virtually excluded from the 'corridors of power' and the TUC is strenuously seeking a new role and the organization to support that role. Its members are concerned with and are part of the 'material' climate of the 1990s and do not want to be excluded from this, but are also concerned with ensuring and participating in the future of the trades union movement. The TUC has set up a review body to consider its way forward, in the face of declining union membership and government hostility. Some unions, such as the EEPTU (Electrical, Engineering and Plumbing Trades Union), feel that the way forward is through change and by adopting 'no strike' and single-union deals in the market place, while others cling to their ideologies and resist change. The expulsion of the EEPTU by the TUC at the Annual Congress in 1988 illustrates clearly the dilemma. At the centre is seen to be the issue of 'poaching' (based on the Bridlington agreement), as one of the main ideological planks of the TUC is that no member can be recruited from another union. The expulsion may be seen also as the move towards a different philosophy. A straw in this particular wind may be the changes in the GMB (General Municipal Boilermakers), particularly in recent initiatives to recruit more women and relate to the changing needs of members. The encouragement of white-collar mergers and sections is another indication of this.

On an optimistic note, many people do feel that there is a valid potential and actual role for the TUC. A major element of this should include a concern with the implications of a single and united Europe, and working with the European Trade Union Confederation. Such developments will include attention to rights and conditions of work and worker participation, with implications for a range of industries and services including library and information services. Industrial democracy, health and safety, consideration of harmonization and problems of the environment and environmental health are all current issues requiring agreed policies. As a body the TUC could also act as a focus for advice, information and consultancy and provide a range of activities and services for its members. The TUC is aware of this, and an outline of its possible future role was contained in the report of the Special Review Body presented to Congress in 1988. There is also a recognition that the concept of the closed shop may have to change as part of the European dimension. The draft policy document from the Labour Party (1990) also recognizes these shifts in thinking and tries to reflect them through new policies.

'Harmonization' (the welding of blue- and white-collar unions) forms another piece of the jigsaw and is dealt with later in some detail. As part of the change process, the current proposals for the possible merger of the two major public unions, NALGO and the TGWU, would produce a strong base as opposition to government policies towards the public sector. Other discussions on merging existing small unions into larger generic unions, mirroring the economic scene in some ways, are also having implications on conditions of service for a range of workers, previously fragmented for negotiating purposes. This too is an issue for the TUC.

Some of these factors can be related quite clearly to library and information services and situations. As tensions increase, the cuts begin to bite and the implications of the Local Government and Housing Act begin to have an effect, a Catch-22 situation may begin to emerge. Libraries will need to keep their profiles high on the political agenda, but in so doing will raise questions not only of accountability, but also of cost-effectiveness and performance indicators. Not to raise the profile will mean probable further marginalization and privatization, while to do so will produce the unpleasant scrutiny of bodies such as the Audit Commission. They will also have to manage tensions caused by a move to smaller 'local' units, yet with increasing central political control. Blue-collar workers may find this situation more straightforward, as jobs in this sector can sometimes be considered in a more prescriptive and quantitative framework. At the same time the concepts of Efficiency, Effectiveness and Economy are being replaced by the 'three C's' – competent, caring and competitive – in relation to value for money. In the education sector, and particularly higher education, the change to corporate status for the polytechnics has produced some of the same tensions, affecting library and information services. This move, with institutions of higher education now functioning side-by-side with local authorities, has had implications for conditions of service and the negotiating machinery. Existing negotiating rights for teachers will be an important benchmark watched by other negotiating bodies, including those affecting the profession. The effects of LMS on pay and conditions of service for teachers will also cause currents between national and local agreements. Current concerns with changes in conditions of employment in the education sector as a result of the Education Reform Act (1988) were highlighted by industrial disputes in 1989 and 1990. The removal of further education from local authority control will also produce tension and change in organizational relationships in this sector.

Also in education, known landmarks such as security of tenure are vanishing with resultant effects on organizational structures and behaviour, and employee uncertainty. Rapid demographic changes and growth in the student population will also contribute to this dynamic. The spotlight will be focused on costs, efficiency, staffing, performance indicators (not necessarily service indicators), performance-related pay, accountability and issues relating to qualitative measurement. Quality versus expansion will produce further difficulties and debates. Changes in power bases contribute to changes in attitudes, and again need an understanding of the processes which are involved. The machinery has been set up to discuss and negotiate industrial relations in the polytechnics, now they have left the maintained public sector. National versus local agreements will have to be considered, including conditions for academic, support, manual and craft employees. There will be a 'knock-on' effect on conditions of service in further education, as negotiations and settlements see-saw between the two.

These changes will have a strong impact on the group dynamics of many workplaces. Those sharing a workplace, with roles and values which are perceived as shared, sometimes see change and development as a threat and so coalesce as anti-management forces, in opposition to what may be seen as the common enemy. Changes in political aims, ideologies and 'outputs' may also cause groups to form and re-form in defensive positions, depending on the parent organization, the status of official and unofficial groups, and what are seen as rules and guidelines. New technology may well be the most obvious area where workers feel threatened and so react in a variety of ways. This is linked to the need for managers to understand the behavioural aspects of workers in a wide framework, and to relate management styles and practices to a range of organizational environments. A concern with the process of relationships will reflect an increasing emphasis on and concern with organizational behaviour.

Many of the current changes, confusions and tensions indicated earlier are transferred in one way or another to the workplace. Personal worries and uncertainties about boundaries and security are reflected in changing and uncertain social groupings. Individuals seek to transfer their insecurities to the organization and so unconsciously look for a 'bad' organization or 'bad' manager with whom their aggression can be located. The emotional development of the young child and organizational development have strong parallels with each other and with psycho-analytical processes. These underline the foundation of all employee relationships and also illustrate the need to begin to understand and develop self-awareness. This issue and others are discussed at more length in the following chapters.

Further reading

ACAS, *Annual report 1988*, London, ACAS, 1989.
ACAS, *Annual report 1989*, London, ACAS, 1990.
Audit Commission, *Economy, efficiency and effectiveness*, London, Audit Commission, 1984.
Education Reform Act, London, HMSO, 1988.
Financing our public library service: four subjects for debate, London, HMSO, 1988, (Green Paper: Cm 324).
Local Government and Housing Act 1989, London, HMSO, 1989.
Purcell, J., *Good industrial relations: theory and practice*, London, Macmillan, 1981.
Removing barriers to employment: proposals for further reform of industrial relations and trade union law, London, HMSO, 1989 (Cm 655).
Special Review Body, *First report*, London, TUC, 1988.
Training for employment, London, HMSO, 1988.
Widdicombe, D., *The conduct of local authority business: report of the Committee of Enquiry*, London, HMSO, 1986 (Cmnd 7797–9801).

Part One

The working environment: contexts and issues

Rosemary Raddon

Introduction to Part One

This part, as explained in the Introduction, focuses on some of the major issues currently affecting people at work. They have been identified as issues which concern all managers, and particularly those in the public sector. They include race, gender, harmonization, performance related pay, performance indicators, and the underlying support structures. These outline the negotiating machinery and process, and counselling and psychodynamic elements. References to further reading are given, and managers' notes are provided at the end of each section.

1 Race

In social and human relationship terms, race issues are sometimes linked to those of gender, particularly in areas of low skilled employment where many ethnic minority and black people are employed. Institutionalized racism works in a variety of ways, including structures and services. For example, many black people join a union as this is perceived as one way of obtaining protection from injustice in the workplace, but few obtain senior positions in union organizations. The same inequalities occur in library and information services.

These are reflections of the social tensions in the British workforce which affect general employee relationships, as well as specific race issues. These tensions have their roots in social and educational issues. Ethnic and black minority groups are disadvantaged educationally and many members under-achieve, due in part to the inbuilt indices of failure in the education system, such as language bias, teacher bias, examination results, and difficulties of access to further and higher education. The process is completed by employment bias and structures. Social deprivation, such as housing and health, compounds the situation. Monitoring of the workforce for this concept is still the exception rather than the rule, and so the under-representation of ethnic and black people in senior positions in either the private or the public sector is difficult to establish in statistical terms. However, where monitoring has been carried out, this under-representation is crystal clear, and so spills over into workplace tensions and antipathy. Harmonization may help to redress this balance a little but is far from being accepted universally and will not placate the grievances of the large numbers of black and ethnic workers in predominantly unskilled and low-grade jobs. The same issue is reflected in union membership – figures are quite high but only at membership level. These figures reflect the need for members of these groups to help prevent further institutionalized racism by participating in middle and senior management in unions, education, local government and industry. In the current economic climate units in some local authorities which are concerned with monitoring discrimination are being abandoned, and this is making the situation even more difficult. These are political rather than managerial decisions.

Social, economic and political imbalances are clearly reflected in the work place and have a marked effect on the industrial relations of black and ethnic-minority workers. The effects of new technology are increasingly felt by these workers as many hold jobs at the lowest levels, lack skills, and are slow to take up training opportunities because of previous experiences of institutionalized racism. This perpetuation of a section of 'have nots' in the community is not a force for development.

The Race Relations Act (1976)[1] is intended to provide enforcement of equal opportunity, supported by the Commission for Racial Equality, which has greater powers than the previously established Race Relations Board. It is concerned with direct and indirect discrimination, based on grounds of colour, race, nationality, ethnic or national origins. Such discrimination is unlawful in major areas, such as employment, education, housing, and the provision of goods and services.

The Act followed the 1965 and 1968 Acts, and reflected changes in social awareness, and particularly discriminatory practices occurring in employment. (It does not cover immigration practices.) It also echoes the concern with sexual equality and with the legislation in the 1975 Sex Discrimination Act.[2] The Equal Opportunities Commission parallels the Commission for Racial Equality, and both try to prevent discrimination.

The Sex Discrimination Act and the Race Relations Act must be seen in relation to the other contemporary issues outlined in the Introduction. Definitions of discrimination appear at the end of the section on Legislation but are also appropriate here.

Direct discrimination involves less favourable treatment than that given to anyone else in the same circumstances.

Indirect discrimination relates to a condition or requirement which means that the person or group who can comply with it, of a specific colour, race or ethnic or national origin, is smaller than the proportion of other persons to do so.

Racism equals power, and this issue cannot easily be denied. The implications in relation to libraries and information services cover many aspects of services, but include policies, planning, structures, resources, stock, recruitment and the implementation and monitoring of an equal opportunities policy. In many cases such policies have been shown to be merely slogans, and are not supported by real practices.

In recruitment terms it is important that the processes of recruitment do follow accepted procedures and that these are monitored at every stage. Statistics will provide supporting facts. Criteria must be defined, shortlisting carried out according to these criteria, and candidates shortlisted and appointed only if they fulfil these, regardless of age, gender, race or religious or sexual preferences. It is important that candidates from minority groups are appointed in accordance with a clear system, with policies and planned services, and are not marginalized and given posts which are inferior to others in the structure. A full equal opportunities policy ensures that all staff are appointed as an integral part of a service, and are not 'attached' through a managerial structural device, which isolates them, and at the same time highlights their 'difference'. Marginalization also encourages the scapegoating of workers by other parts of the organization. Services which emanate from such marginalization are also seen to be of less importance than other services, and the users perceive this. The gap between the planners and users then quickly widens, and it is inevitably racial and other minorities who withdraw very quickly, both physically and mentally, from services which are seen to be notional. Once a differential approach has been identified, in practice, structure or service, then it becomes increasingly difficult to establish communication and good relationships with the users. The confidence and morale of other staff is then affected, producing a downward spiral. This applies to the public sector, but also to education services, health and welare, social information work and other areas. Distance in the key relationship between user and librarian or information worker then prevents effective communication and planning.

Finance and financial planning is a major issue which relates to race, and many black activists see section 11 funding, for example, as a way of also marginalizing library services to black and ethnic minorities. As well as being a political statement, this attitude does reflect the point that specific staff, structures and services are often not integrated into 'mainstream' services, and so are external to the total concept. They are not within the pattern of McKinsey's 'shared values'. Staff development and training are the ultimate key issues, as without shifts in attitudes and understanding, real change will not occur in services. Information is an important element, but understanding and attitudes are much more difficult to effect and even more difficult to measure. There are many parallels here with gender and in both cases the issue of power is the underlying concern. Power is linked in turn with control, and so with the tensions between the traditional paternalistic and centralist patterns of service provision, the move towards decentralization, and the central political dislike of local-government power bases. Again many black activists perceive this local authority power as another way of disguising racism. Services delivered by a predominantly white bureaucracy are not seen to reflect the needs of minority and black groups.

Managing the tensions and shifts in policy and service delivery is difficult and requires great sensitivity, as well as understanding of the underlying emotions which produce these tensions. These include unacknowledged fears within the workforce, not only in economic and social terms, but those which relate to unconscious fears and worries. These are then, in psychodynamic terms, 'split off' from the individual, and projected into the person or group who then has to carry the anger and fear. In service terms this means that 'peripheral' departments concerned with services to racial minority groups become even more isolated from what are perceived as mainstream services. There is a clear need to relate services to ideologies, and for the manager to understand these relationships.

References
1 *Race Relations Act*, London, HMSO, 1976.
2 *Sex Discrimination Act*, London, HMSO, 1975 (Amendment 1986).

Further reading
Braham, P., Rhodes, E. and Pearn, M. (eds.), *Discrimination and disadvantage in employment*, London, Hayer and Ren, 1981.
Burrington, G. *Equal opportunities in librarianship? gender and career aspirations*, London, Library Association Publishing, 1987.
Commission for Racial Equality, *Code of practice for the elimination of racial discrimination*, London, CRE, 1983.
Commission for Racial Equality, *Review of the Race Relations Act 1976: proposals for changes*, London, CRE, 1985.
Ellis, V., *The role of trade unions in the promotion of equal opportunities*, Manchester, EOC and Social Science Research Council, 1981.
'Equal opportunities 1988', *Library Association record*, **91** (1), 1989, 33–4.
Equal Opportunities Commission, *Equality at work: a guide to the employment provisions of the Sex Discrimination Act 1975*, Manchester, EOC, 1982.
Hunt, A. (ed.), *Women and paid work: issues of equality*, London, Macmillan, 1988.
Lewis, J. (ed.), *Women's welfare, women's rights*, London, Croom Helm, 1983.
Library Association, *Equal opportunities information pack*, London, LA, 1989.
Local Authorities Conditions of Service Advisory Board, *Equal opportunities and employment: a brief summary of the law*, London, LACSAB, 1985 (Employers' guide no. 10).
Macdonald, I., *Race relations: the new law*, London, Butterworth, 1977.
Palmer, C. and Poulton, K., *Sex and race discrimination in employment*, London, Legal Action Group, 1988.

Trades Union Congress, *Black workers' charter*, London, TUC, 1987.
Trades Union Congress, *Education and training of girls and women*, London, TUC, 1987.
Trades Union Congress, *Trade unions and black workers*, London, TUC, 1986.
Trades Union Congress, *Working women*, London, TUC, 1983.

Manager's notes

Be able to define racism
Be able to recognize racism in all its forms
Read the legislation and identify main issues
Ensure policies, practices, structures and services are not discriminatory
Involve the workforce
Manage practices
Monitor practices

2 Gender

Issues of gender and race can be clearly identified in relation to organizational change, while class issues are more diffuse. Political shifts have of course affected women, with left-wing governments in general much more sympathetic to the ideal of equal working rights for women, child-care facilities, and full benefits and recognition from the State of women's issues. The importance of the issue of child-care facilities has now been recognized by the GMB (see Part Two) and also by the TUC. The universal provision of facilities has been identified as a long-term goal. There is an increase in the number of women, many of whom are married, in full- and part-time paid employment, for a range of reasons. These include economic conditions, patterns of social change and heightened social and political awareness. But the fact remains that the vast majority of women still work in unskilled or second-tier jobs, with rapid turnover. The working patterns of women differ sharply from those of men, for reasons which have been well articulated, including attitudes, stereotyping, expectations, curriculum bias, discriminatory practices, discriminatory legislation, social pressures, plus limited access to workplace training and education, and other factors.

Women have a pattern of work which is frequently punctuated by periods out of the labour market (child rearing, caring for elderly relatives), while men present a pattern of much more continuous employment, and with more viability. Social and economic conditions will change patterns, but the issue is a pertinent one for unions and union membership. Women are also clustered in a smaller number of industries, as well as in the caring professions, and overall tend to cluster in what are perceived as predominantly 'female' occupations. The dual labour market, with distinctions between the considerable numbers of women in low-paid and low-skilled jobs and the few in highly paid jobs, reinforces the difference between this and the other market sector, with predominantly male and highly paid workers. Yet despite the complex legislation and changing ideology, the small numbers of women in more senior positions remains virtually unchanged. However, current alterations in the balance and distribution of the workforce are now producing changes in conditions of work and expectations. For blue-collar and professional workers, increasing concern with conditions of work, as well as job satisfaction and good relationships within the work context, have become important. This participation has produced reactions to the male-dominated power bases, again changing the dynamics of group relationships.

New technology may have and may be contributing to the de-skilling of some of the work of women. The paradox here is that in some areas, such as the clothing industry, new technology has de-skilled male workers, through the introduction of computer programs to design and cut materials, for example. At the same time, advanced techniques in sales and marketing information have led to ever-increasing demands for fashion changes, thus supporting the home worker, often exploited but necessary to the consumer outlets. The majority of these workers are, of course, women. Technology has also begun to play a positive role. It could be argued that at present the advantages are confined to the relatively privileged but these should in time have a spin-off for all women. Support is being built up through networking and providing information on skills training, job and career possibilities. Areas of expertise, resource banks and databases are growing fast, and as in librarianship and information services, these overlap and relate to other disciplines. Negative aspects of the new technology relate to the repetitive jobs in industry and the replacement of traditional skills, such as those in the furniture and clothing industries, with computer-aided design and execution. The developing countries, where women often form the major workforce, are being severely affected by these developments, as traditional sources of expertise and production are being replaced. This affects the economic balance of such communities.

In the union movement itself, women are in general seriously under-represented, and this reflects the general gender bias of the workplace. Women also hold few senior positions in most unions and in the TUC. In male-dominated unions this underlines social and class attitudes. In relation to the workplace it is part of the complex socio-economic scene where again women are in a 'no win' situation, as far as some members are concerned. Press too far for the cause of women's rights and organizations will react in the time-honoured way by 'withdrawing' into themselves. Try and achieve some of the apparently desirable male norms and characteristics, and the goal-posts are constantly moved or, if they are not, women who reach stronger positions in organizations are seen by other women to have totally espoused the male world. This in turn produces psychological pressures on women in senior positions, and the stress on them is considerable. Expectations, language, role models and male perceptions are all pressures on women, requiring self-analysis, strength and confidence to reject male norms and values. These pressures apply to women in the library and information profession. In some quarters this pressure is recognized, with a growth in counselling and psychotherapy services particularly concerned with gender issues. Many women are seeking a recognition of their own qualities, and want organizations to respect and reflect these, which in turn will produce role models for those entering changing organizations. Training, facilities, relevance and flexibility all need to be implemented if women are to play a stronger role. Low status and low perception do not encourage women to hold office. It is crucial that women are represented in the unions, as they need to be carrying out policy-making and negotiating conditions of work – both from an informed feminine viewpoint.

Equal opportunities are another area of concern for women where there is a need for policies to be supported by *real* practices, and monitored effectively to see if the policies and practices do actually work. Cross-cultural practices come into play here, as many women who are suffering acute discrimination are from ethnic and black minorities, disadvantaged socially and economically, but also excluded either overtly or covertly from the union movement.

Current privatization developments and the implementation of CCT (competitive contract tendering) will also have an effect on women who will no longer be able to enjoy advantages negotiated for them by local authorities, such as flexible working hours, job share and maternity leave. Any new negotiations will have to take note of the needs of women, but may be difficult to negotiate and to implement, particularly in the current climate.

The support of unions and industrial tribunals is also important to women in relation to areas such as sexual harassment at work, where such practices are well known but the machinery for changing and challenging the accepted order may not be so well known.

Industrial tribunals, backed up by the legislation, do provide some support, but individuals need far more support and information than is generally available. However, the legislative framework does provide a base, and can act as a safety net, particularly if unions embrace it in a positive rather than a negative way. (Legislation can also be used as a blocking device to prevent women progressing.) Legislation and tribunals can also affect the long-term aspirations of women in low-paid work. For example, changes in the Health Service are providing opportunities for women to take grievances to tribunals, and so litigation is eventually going to affect pay, and this in turn will have an effect on structures. So again organizational change will have to be managed as a result of changing forces. Women will change their position in the hierarchy. The male-dominated organization will no longer be seen as the norm.

Gender issues in library and information services relate in the main to structure, style, services, resources and personnel practices. These issues are reflected in the way in which women are represented at senior levels of management, and the way in which their contributions are perceived by those who provide (or not) structures which allow women to make valid contributions to organizational development. Services must be of value, and marginalization must be avoided. In the public sector users may prefer resources and services of particular concern to women to be clearly identified, while others may find this irrelevant – decisions will depend on local circumstances and need. The important issue is that such decisions should not be made in a condescending and paternalistic way by senior managers, without consulting and communicating with the consumer.

Resources are another important element. Bias needs to be recognized and taken in context, and cannot be ignored in relation to resource provision. Information for and about gender issues must be available, and information on health provision, education, support networks and groups distributed and made available in ways and places that are suitable to the needs of women. Language in relation to gender issues is also important – in the choice and use of language, and its relationship to the information carrier and intended audience. It is also important in structural terms and in recruitment practices.

Recruitment issues parallel those which relate to race, and structures and policies will reflect policies. Again monitoring will provide hard facts and not just opinions. Monitoring will also provide statistics on women who are doubly disadvantaged – those who are female and from minority groups. Stereotyping and discrimination must be removed from recruitment practices. These practices and processes have to be monitored at all stages: this includes the job analysis (including the legislative boundaries), job description, person specification, advertisement, shortlisting, interview process, terms of employment and probationary conditions. Monitoring includes the collection of statistical data, and should also involve consideration of the language used in these processes.

Statistics on the library and information profession in relation to women in positions of senior management are as illuminating as those for the teaching profession: a profession which is predominantly female is represented by a senior elite which is predominantly male. This illustrates the issues of attitude, expectations and all the related complexities of a male-dominated society. Equal opportunities policies are needed to help redress the balance, plus strong legislation and effective monitoring systems.

Many women in library and information services also lack role models, and this can undermine confidence. Many organizations also conform to traditional practices and attitudes, and so do not provide child-care facilities or support women working in ways which enable them to care for children or elderly relatives. At the same time women in senior positions in some structures are also expected to join in traditional after-work drinking and social habits. This is another double bind: to join in is to negate personal feelings and to reject such activities is seen as elitist or remote.

Organizational development in most services is also based on traditional norms and values, but there is a need to define and feed into the planning cycle women's perceptions of management styles and organizational development. Information on women's attitudes and aspirations form part of management and organizational development. This needs to be as a result of collaborative work, not the imposition of one set of stereotyped ideas on another set of workers. The imposition of male concepts of compensatory training and development are equally invalid. Genuine interaction and sharing of ideas can produce genuine change.

Regardless of the context in which women work in the library and information profession, all changes have to be backed up by staff training and development. In areas of attitude change, a crucial element in relation to gender, there is a need for sensitivity as well as information. Changing perceptions and ideas cannot be limited to skills training, for example, as they bring a need to re-assess and re-consider the totality of an organization, not just its services or resources. All the issues indicated earlier are involved, from new technology to child care. Team-building, counselling and networking can all provide support for women involved in this process. There is ample scope for further research on employment practice, attitudes and the effects of legislation on women in employment, as well as on their support and information needs.

Further reading

Allen, R., *How to prepare a case for an industrial tribunal*, 2nd ed., Manchester, EOC, 1987.

Apslund, G., *Women managers: changing organisational cultures*, London, Wiley, 1988.

Ellis, V., *The role of trade unions in the promotion of equal opportunities*, Manchester, EOC and Social Science Research Council, 1981.

'Equal opportunities 1988', *Library Association record*, **91** (1), 1989, 33-4.

Equal Opportunities Commission, *Code of practice*, Manchester, EOC, 1985.

Equal Opportunities Commission, *Equal treatment of men and women: strengthening the acts*, Manchester, EOC, 1988.

Hammond, V., 'Men and women managers: the challenge of working together', *Women and training news*, 5, 1981,

'How far has the company equality gone?', *Labour research*, **77** (12), 1989, 11-13.

Library Association, *Equal opportunities information pack*, London, LA, 1989.

Marshall, J., *Women managers: travellers in a male world*, Chichester, Wiley, 1984.

Ritchie, S., 'Women in library management', in Vaughan, A. (ed.), *Studies in library management*, Vol. 7, London, Bingley, 1982.

Sex Discrimination Act, London, HMSO, 1975 (Amendment 1986).

Thomas, R. R., 'From affirmative action to affirming diversity', *Harvard business review*, **68** (2), 1970, 107-17.

Trades Union Congress, *Black and ethnic-minority women in employment and trade unions*, London, TUC, 1987.

Trades Union Congress, *Education and training of girls and women*, London, TUC, 1987.

Trades Union Congress, *Women in the labour market*, London, TUC, 1983.

Walby, S., *General segregation at work*, Milton Keynes, Open University, 1988.

Manager's notes

Understand the issues and supporting legislation
Identify major issues relating to gender in the organization
Establish policies
Establish structures

**Plan long-term and short-term changes
Involve the workforce
Implement and support change
Monitor practices**

3 Harmonization

The improvement of personnel and industrial relations in the workplace has been given added impetus in recent years by the concept of 'harmonization', or 'the single-status workforce' or 'standardization'. All are terms which are part of a movement towards the establishment of common policies and practices, particularly in the area of conditions of service. This move aims to cross the divide of 'white-collar' and 'manual' staff, so that the harmonization of the workforce, or standardization of conditions, applies to *all* workers. This will affect organizational decisions in library and information services, and also salaries, career expectations, and staff development policies.

Some definitions may be helpful here:

Staff status: all workers to be assimilated into terms and conditions of service which operate for staff.

Harmonization: the implementation of a common approach to pay and conditions of service. This seeks to *reduce* differences within various categories of employees.

Single status: a policy which adopts common standards and practices for all employees in an organization.

Some of the issues referred to earlier are pertinent to harmonization, including the need for the implementation of current economic policies. These are part of the changing context, and include the single-union discussions that have been taking place recently, as a direct result of changing commercial ideas. Other current factors, such as work patterns and expectations, stress on service and leisure industries, mobility of staff and demographic changes, will support the need for greater efficiency in the workplace. They will also help remove the need for time wasting and artificially and socially imposed demarcation lines. In library and information services these have focused on the lower-paid and less-skilled jobs, but the boundaries will become increasingly blurred. Workers will be able to take on added responsibilities and so will question working practices. Gender issues will also be relevant, as many of the women coming back to work, either having had or expecting further training, will be aware of gender inequalities and unwilling to accept these in the 1990s. Reorganization in local government, including the 'three Es' as well as the 'three Cs', another factor, as is compulsory competitive tendering, which aims to provide an economic service, rather than support post-war ideologies such as 'the right to work'. This in turn reflects current attitudes towards unions and unionization. Performance assessment and performance-related pay are also important, as these ideas will cut across status lines, especially now that pilot schemes for performance-related pay are being introduced at senior levels in local government and elsewhere.

Such developments link with the original social and educational reasons for the differences, when a small elite class could reward and manage a larger labour force, in a relatively rigid society. These are now changing rapidly, and so the moves towards harmonization are reflecting these changes.

The concept is still in a relatively early stage of development, and subject to union and employers' discussions and negotiations. Although the removal of differential practices and conditions is the long-term goal, there may be some differences which unions wish to maintain. This means that an approach to such policies can totally embrace the idea, or can approach it from establishing, and then removing, the reasons and practices for differences. Some organizations and unions take the former approach, some the latter, and some an overlapping combination of the two. But the need to establish and agree common policies and ideologies is the underlying reason for any moves in this direction. Barriers will include the attitudes of some organizations and cultures towards the idea, tensions between groups of employees, often as a result of social insecurities and attitudes, inter-union differences, and the complicated bargaining machinery which currently exists. This will eventually have to be integrated into a local level of negotiation if it is to progress.

An organization or service involved in single-status moves needs to be clear about the advantages involved, ensure that the workforce is aware of these, and so provide adequate information and consultation on the process. It must also establish overall policies. Finance must be available, and the organization be in a state which enables it to encompass and absorb change. The bureaucratic procedures, including the negotiating machinery, must also be able to cope with change. Staff may be uneasy if these policies are implemented without due care, because they will impinge on personal insecurities. These insecurities may be fundamental psycho-dynamic issues, or the more obvious ones of class, status and, in many cases, race. Union representatives may consciously or unconsciously manipulate the situation, and the same issues may be involved. In some cases unions may wish to perpetuate the differences, to maintain the existence of 'an opposing force', which, as explained in the section on psychodynamic issues and elsewhere, fulfils an important focus for negative feelings, recognized or unrecognized.

Salaries versus pay or wages, conditions of service, such as hours of work and holidays, as well as sick pay and career opportunities, are all important and related elements in the situation. The methods of determining pay are also important and have status connotations. In library and information services this applies clearly to library assistants versus clerical staff, and word-processing operatives versus graphic designers. These differences are then mirrored by the collective bargaining machinery and union structure in relation to the occupations. They range from local schemes to national bargaining structures (outlined in a later section) but these too reflect the relative status of occupations. Women in the lower-paid posts and manual workers, for example, will expect training so that they can progress beyond clerical and typing grades. The structure and salaries of library assistants will then be affected. The tradition of routine posts being held by staff unable to take on more responsibilities will be challenged. This in turn will challenge middle management, and team librarianship and team building take on a different perspective. The organization will then need to restructure some of the areas of responsibility.

The processes of harmonization are interesting in terms of organizational and personnel relations because of the reflection of social issues and the changes in historical concepts. Tensions have and will arise as a result of these changes. Further tensions may well arise in workplaces as further changes take place. Technological and economic developments may, however, force the pace over the retention and organization of personnel, and decide the time-scale and patterns of implementation.

Further reading
ACAS, *Developments in harmonisation*, London, ACAS, 1982 (Discussion paper no. 1).
Greater London Joint Council for Local Authorities Services (Manual Workers), Joint Secretariat, *Harmonisation and single status – joint GLJC guidelines*, London, GLJC, nd.
Institute of Personnel Management, *Staff status for all*, London, IPM, 1977.
TUC, *Industrial democracy*, London, TUC, 1974.

Manager's notes

*Be familiar with the concept of harmonization
Establish policies if appropriate to your organization
Plan for long-term and short-term changes
Make sure the workforce understands these – communicate and inform
Implement change in consultation with all agencies involved*

4 Performance indicators and performance-related pay

Employee relationships will be affected by any change in an organization, whether these changes occur as a result of political or economic forces, or as a result of changing internal objectives and inter- and intra-group dynamics. Such events need not be mutually exclusive, and performance indicators, linked to performance-related pay, are two important current examples. Both produce a climate of uncertainty and so affect relationships – for example, group to group, small group to large group, social groups, task groups, individual to individual, and individual to hierarchy.

In the context of the changing environment outlined in the Introduction, performance indicators are assuming increasing importance, as they are used to help assess the achievement, or not, of aims and objectives, the extent of that achievement, and to make comparisons between services. They also relate to the concept of accountability. The optimal use of resources, including people, is a key issue. There may, however, be conflicts between criteria established centrally by the government and those established locally – particularly evident in the education sector. For example, research, citations and publications are criteria of excellence valued by universities, but not necessarily accepted in relation to funding recognition. The attempt to measure performance against a predetermined set of indicators makes the concept of performance-related pay equally valid. The concept supports the ethos of a market-driven economy, rather than that of employment (and education) as social processes fulfilling social needs. In terms of personal relationships, these needs are important, as they reflect, add to or detract from individual needs in relation to upbringing, emotional support and unconscious drives, which are manifested through patterns of behaviour at work. These then have to be 'picked up' and managed by those with relevant responsibilities. The implementation of performance-related pay involves shifts in managerial techniques, attitudes and understanding. The implementation of performance-related staff-appraisal schemes, as one area of application, requires training, communication and the involvement of all those concerned. It also involves the application of staff development systems as part of continuing professional development. Appraisal in terms of merit or worth opens up considerable areas of personal insecurity and has to be handled sensitively. The need for improved counselling, guidance and training of employers and employees is the important corollary. The private and the public sectors can each adapt the skills of the other to develop the process.

Performance indicators and performance measurement have been managerial tools for many years, and a subject of warm debate since the 1960s. The changes outlined earlier have added impetus to the issue, and in the public sector accountability has been a strong factor. Services which are to be considered 'value for money', as well as economical, efficient and effective, have to be measured in some way to determine if such goals have been met. The debate over quantitative and qualitative factors then becomes valid, and in the context of library and information services the recent green paper on public library services,[1] and the Education Reform Act (1988)[2] have added political impetus to the situation.

The Further Education Unit (FEU)[3,4] is an example of one body that has responded to the debate, and has used the curriculum and curriculum change to establish criteria and use these as a base for measurement. The Chartered Institute of Public Finance and Accountancy (CIPFA)[5] and the Audit Commission[6] have also produced indicators of service, as well as the Jarratt Committee[7] for higher education. The Office of Arts and Libraries (OAL)[8] is currently working on indicators for services. The difficulty of producing precise, measurable and meaningful indicators is evident. Pollitt[9] has argued that this approach (outputs) does not take into account other factors, such as respect, availability or involvement. The complex issues of what is wanted (or needed) by the users are pushed into the background.

These debates between qualitative and quantitative measurements have not been resolved in other areas, notably the social services, medicine, and law and order. Analysis of need in order to plan services may clash with political ideologies and so affect funding. This again produces difficulties for employees, whose personal ideologies may differ from the organizational or corporate ideologies, and who may then project their unease, dislike or anger onto convenient 'parent figures' in the organization. Difficulties also have to be resolved over the actual measurement, i.e. the whole job, or part of the job, and the machinery for appraisal. These cross currents can affect output and make the concept of 'shared values' very difficult to achieve. Management can easily become the common enemy, and then interpersonal relationships are very complex. 'Hidden' agendas, projections and power struggles then become the real issue, rather than that of deciding corporately on aims and objectives, indicators for these, and measuring their achievement.

Some issues relate specifically to the library and information profession, and relationships need to be explored in this particular context. The history of the efforts to produce performance indicators for library and information services has been well documented by Goodall.[10] The debate has been alive for a considerable time, and the difficulties mirror many of those in the world of education, but without the impetus of the Education Reform Act. There are also similarities in management terms. It is difficult to provide an atmosphere in which staff feel they can contribute to the establishment of the organization's aims and objectives when the profession is still defining these in the overall context. Any measurement underlines the nature of this debate, and so impetus may come from political sources rather than from professional ideologies. This in turn weakens structures so that insecurities among individuals and groups become more evident. These insecurities can be manifested in all sorts of ways, and relate to age, personal circumstances and so on, but will be more discernible in a climate of unease.

Specific measurable and measured data have long been used by library and information services, but relating to services rather than people. These data have been used for internal and external measurements and comparisons. In some places, such as Surrey, performance reviews have been clearly linked to service reviews and long-term planning and changes, but again in the context of political initiatives. These data are part of management-information systems, but to ensure involvement, staff have to 'own' the design of the system as well as the collection of data. Divorce from this process will be perceived as a threat, and in weak areas as an example of all-pervasive management being uncaring about the needs of the individual worker. Again, the concept of management as the good or bad parent is pertinent.

Data also have to be seen in the Audit Commission's brief of 'economy', 'efficiency' and 'effectiveness', again with particular reference to the public sector. The recent performance indicators proposed by the Universities Funding Committee and the PCFC are very similar, concerned with costs, student numbers, staff/student ratios, examination results, employment success and wastage figures. These have to be seen in relation to an institutional framework. In this context library measurements of efficiency are seen in costs of input and output and the ratio of resources and costs to student numbers. Definitions of these terms may well be helpful, but have also to be related to 'conventional wisdom' in that there are some areas of library and information services that are difficult to measure. These include professional expertise in the area of relating to the individual, in a personal rather than in a cost effective way. The latter does not entirely fit into the commercial concept of market-led services, and there are tensions here between 'costs', 'professionalism' and 'need'. Interpersonal and organizational responses can also differ here. Workers who feel threatened in any way will produce their own defence mechanisms, and in the context of the profession these often relate to complex bureaucratic proceedings. They serve as a protection against issues which are seen to be unpleasant or threatening, such as market forces or accountability.

Efficiency can be seen as relating to the relationship of input to output, or the increase in output with a constant input. Effectiveness relates to the relationship between outputs and objectives. The objectives will often relate to the needs of the end user. The measurement of the outcome of this relationship may be as difficult to measure as the outcome of a successful diagnosis from the interaction between client and dentist through using effective technical support, such as the X-ray machine.

Measures identified so far can be grouped together. These can include input and output statistics, processes, including the so-called user-education process, stock organization, response times to demand, use of services, and the relationship or effect on the user or consumer. All these have pertinent methods of collecting and testing data, but must be seen clearly as techniques. The danger is that they become ends in themselves and tools for personal protection. The sensitive manager must recognize these protective processes and understand them. The opinion of the consumer, obtained through market-research techniques or through measurable demand, is another area of measurement. Quality and relevance may, however, be crude indicators on the part of the user.

Performance-related pay can be seen as an area in which measures are applied to the producer of services or goods, rather than as a measure of satisfaction by the consumer. Pay is based on the notional concept of performance and so there is a need for measures to be evolved which link the two. A balance has to be maintained between rewarding the group, the team and the individual, and the health of the organization. The size, scale and proportion of pay have to be determined, or the approach in determining pay. (This must be distinguished from job evaluation, which is a process which decides the pay for a specific job, but is not concerned with the way in which that job is, or is not, effected.)

A target approach can be considered, in which pay is related to attainable and measurable targets. In relation to performance indicators in library and information services, this can be an increase in issues, queries solved, speed of document-delivery times etc. The difficulties relate to the extent to which the person being measured can, in real terms, affect what is happening in total. A query, for example, may be answered by reference to another source, specialist database, or simple personal knowledge, depending on the complexity of the question. The 'value' of the answer is difficult to measure. So where does the accolade for the 'solving' lie? Boundaries become blurred and individual responsibilities difficult to pin down. This can result in antagonism, bureaucratic 'economy with the truth', an overloading of some systems and people, and so on.

Leading from this, pay could be related to teamwork, and could be used to improve teamwork. Again indicators are needed but may be difficult to define as they are subjective. Within a team different levels of performance may be rewarded, which in turn leads to the need for definitions again. The target for the team could be indicated by the use of words such as 'outstanding', 'effective', or 'good', 'average' and 'bad'. The definitions and the bias of the words present problems, before quantitative measurements are added.

It is also possible to consider the issue from the context of the 'whole job', or applied standards. The definition can then involve stating what the job is about and what qualities are needed to perform it well, such as judgement, initiative, leadership, quantity of output, quality of output, all of which can have, or may have, weighting elements, depending on the circumstances. The procedural issues need to be quite clear and training needs defined, otherwise two people may be involved in difficult delineation of duties. The imposition of artificial boundaries may then be seen as threatening or, on the other hand, may be seen as a security factor.

Measuring different levels of performance, appraising them, providing pay awards and incentives and linking this to staff development, is a circular process which always returns to the question of the way in which the performance is to be assessed.

These elements have also to be seen in a climate of centralized bargaining, the dismantling of traditional negotiating machinery, such as the Burnham procedures for teachers, decreasing union power, market forces, and cash limits. The latter will affect the implementation of performance-related pay, through imposing some rigid parameters.

The concepts from the private sector have been adapted in many cases by the public sector, which was unable to reward high performers, and so in some cases welcomed the 'award' idea, and at the same time enabled organizations not to reward those who were not seen to be performing adequately. Such payment schemes are seen to attract and retain high-quality staff and motivate workers to achieve high performance. All involve improved communication, trained staff to implement them, appropriate contracts and achievable targets. In personal terms, many workers feel such schemes to be fair, and benefit from their involvement. It is much more difficult for the worker involved in such schemes to 'split off' the unpleasant parts and project the anger at boring or unrewarded tasks onto other individuals or groups.

However, there are disadvantages. The pace of change may be too fast, training and counselling may be inadequate, quantifiable criteria may have dominance over qualitative criteria, key tasks only may be considered to the exclusion of others, and there may be a tendency for payment for 'short-term' results, neglecting long-term qualitative considerations. One of the many disadvantages is that such frameworks can be reversed and so stifle innovation and creativity.

In general terms, the attitude of unions towards performance awards is not positive, and schemes tend to flourish most effectively in sectors and industries with a low union representation (not to be confused with profit-sharing and share-owning schemes). The relationships between management and unions will also help determine the level and extent of the schemes. The proportions of workers in specific task areas, the attitudes and relationships of different groups to the reward system, and the policies of management are all affective issues.

This area raises many personal relationship issues, but if performance assessment and performance-related pay are to be taken seriously, such issues must also be taken seriously.

Attitudes towards personal relationships and feelings in this area illustrate good management practice, and can support or detract from effective personal relationships. The process of performance assessment needs to be seen as a positive and constructive initiative, one which contributes to the performance of the individual. It contributes valuable feedback to workers and also provides essential recognition of worth. The review process, if objective and linked to specific developmental goals for individual workers, should help identify reasons for poor performance. These are then viewed positively, so that the necessary training, counselling or development initiatives can be implemented. These initiatives must be carefully matched and not over-generalized. Specific responses can then help redress previous imbalances, particularly in relation to age, sex, status, race or class, and so be very positive. This should form part of a cycle, so that performance appraisal is planned and meaningful, and not just an antagonistic, 'one off' encounter. Jobs and workers have to be seen as unique individuals, and so the process is time-consuming if it really is applied in relation to individual people and individual posts. Other benefits relate to improved communication channels between those being appraised and those carrying out the appraisal.

The organization has to provide a system for appraisal, which as well as being systematic, must fit the culture of the organization and the style of those working in it and managing it. Most important of all, the support network has to be in place and effective, not be just a notional support system. Such an ethos requires personal and financial investment and a clear understanding of relationships. A strong framework is needed to support personal insecurities and projections.

Managers have to understand the processes involved, be aware of their own part in the proceedings, of possible tensions and the dynamics of the situation. They have to plan the procedures well, and also have good observational, listening, caring and counselling skills. They must also be aware of interacting with workers at a very personal level, and touching on personal insecurities, difficulties, projections and complex motivating forces. The presenting issues may mask more subtle behavioural patterns, and understanding these allows a manager not to expect instant change or development. He or she must understand the reasons for apparent inadequacies. The award system must also be clearly defined.

The difficulties lie in the expertise and training of managers and the expectations of employees. The confusion between the concepts of appraisal and reward adds to the difficulties. Psychodynamic forces again come into play, as those doing the appraisals relate to those being appraised: the first links to training and ability, and the second to an attitudinal willingness, interest or desire to be appraised. The motives of and between the two can be complex, involving transference and counter-transference concepts. These issues also need to be seen in relation to those of data collection and analysis, as there is a danger that the process may become unbalanced and so non-productive. Gaps between those involved in research and in designing and collecting the information, and those actually operating the schemes may become too wide. All these aspects produce information which, if used in organizational and individual development, as part of a management-information system, can support a very powerful and flexible workforce.

References
1 *Financing our public library service: four subjects for debate*, London, HMSO, 1988 (Green paper: Cm 324).
2 *Education Reform Act*, London, HMSO, 1988.
3 Further Education Unit, *Quality in NAFE*, London, FEU, 1987.
4 Further Education Unit, *Investing in change: an appraisal of staff development needs for the delivery of modernised occupational training*, London, FEU, 1986.
5 Chartered Institute of Public Finance and Accountancy, *Performance indicators in schools*, London, CIPFA, 1988.
6 Audit Commission, *Improving economy, efficiency and effectiveness in the public sector*, London, Audit Commission, 1983.
7 *Report of the Steering Committee for efficiency studies in universities*, London, Committee of Vide-Chancellors and Principals, 1985 (Jarratt Report).
8 Office of Arts and Libraries, *Keys to success: performance indicators for public libraries. A manual of performance measures and indicators developed by King Research Ltd.* London, HMSO, 1990 (Library Information Series No. 18).
9 Pollitt, C., 'Beyond the managerial model: the case for broadening performance assessment in government and the public services', *Financial accountability and management*, **2** (3), 1986, 155–70.
10 Goodall, D. L., 'Performance measurement: a historical perspective', *Journal of librarianship*, **20** (2), 1988, 128–44.

Further reading
Audit Commission, *Performance review in local government: a handbook for auditors and local authorities*, London, HMSO, 1986.
Committee of Vice-Chancellors and Principals and University Grants Committee, *University management statistics and performance indicators*, London, CVCP, 1988.
Coombe, G., 'Reviewing the situation: performance reviews in Surrey', *Public library journal*, **2** (5), 1987, 76–81.
Fowler, A., 'New directions in performance pay', *Personnel management*, **20** (11), 1988, 30–4.
Kedney, B. and Parkes, D. (eds.), *Planning the F. E. curriculum: implications of the 1988 Education Reform Act*, London, FEU, 1988.
LAMSAC, *Putting performance review into practice*, London, Local Authorities Management Services and Computer Committee, 1979.
Managing colleges efficiently: report of a study of efficiency in non-advanced further education, London, DES/HMSO, 1987.

Raddon, R., 'Question time – public libraries, are they worth it?', *Public library journal*, **3** (6), 1988, 113–17.

Tomkins, C. R., *Achieving economy, efficiency and effectiveness in the public sector*, London, Routledge and Kegan Paul, 1987.

Manager's notes

Clarify the objectives of your organization
Define appropriate performance indicators in relation to the objectives
Decide on the possible grouping of indicators
Identify key indicators (qualitative and/or quantitative) and decide on priorities
Identify how key indicators can be measured. Decide if and how they are related to pay
Determine if and when performance related pay should be implemented
Decide on systems. Implement systems
Involve workforce in all processes
Monitor

5 Conditions of work and the negotiating machinery

The negotiating machinery which applies to local authorities forms the foundation for relationships as well as negotiations. The basis of the machinery is prescriptive and detailed, and is determined by employers and employees. It covers conditions of service for most workers at local, provincial and national levels. It can then be applied equally effectively by both sides of the negotiating table in any particular local circumstances. This joint determination of conditions forms the complementary side of the process. The background is important in relation to changing contexts, particularly issues such as single-union agreements, and rewards which are related to some kind of assessment rather than linked to grade and experience. The machinery is standardized, organized and controlled, and in one way fulfils government philosophy in that it is centrist, but fails in another aspect in that it cannot quickly and easily respond to specific local needs. This rather ambiguous situation is reflected by many employers' view of the situation, while some workers may tend to view the machinery as supportive and providing adequate boundaries. It can also be seen to prevent discrimination, especially against women and part-time workers. The legal rights of trade unionists as well as of employees is part of the picture, and an outline of these is contained in the section on legislation.

The machinery which exists is as follows:

The first tier of negotiations takes place at a national level, with a clear framework for administrative, professional, technical and clerical staff (APT&C). The framework and agreements are enshrined in the *Purple book*.[1] This includes details of all levels and conditions of service. For manual workers the same detail and and guidance for workers and management is contained in the *Buff book*,[2] while conditions for craft workers are contained in the *Green book*.[3] There is also a Joint National Committee for Chief Officers (Principal Officer 6 and above).

The negotiations at national level are conducted via the Local Government Management Board, formed through the merger of the Local Government Training Board (LGTB), and the Local Authorities Conditions of Service Advisory Board (LACSAB). This includes representatives from the local authorities and from the staff side, for manual workers as well as administrative, technical and clerical workers. These employees are represented by the appropriate trade unions and other staff associations. One difficulty is the differences in perceptions between negotiators, or politicians, and managers, which can be evident at this level. LGMB forms part of a national network with the Provincial Councils, comprised of local authority representation (Councillors) and trade-union representation. The Provincial Councils allow good relationships to be developed between local authorities and their employees, and provide a forum for conciliation and arbitration as well as information.

National	Items requiring national resolution	LGMB or Provincial Councils
Provincial	Unresolved issues from local sources	GLES or other regional machinery
Local	Specific issues	Joint local committees

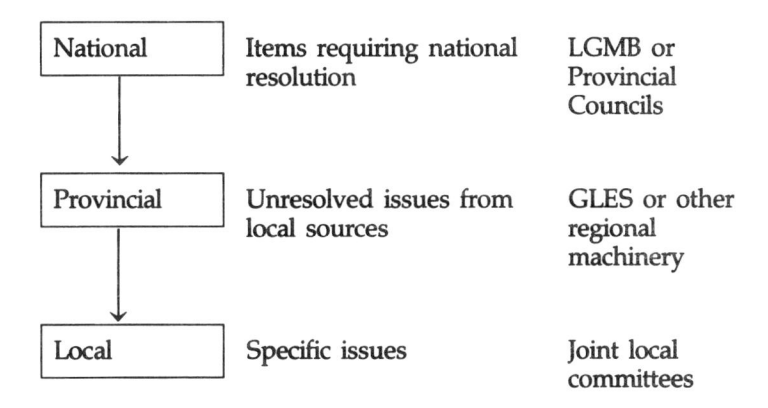

Fig. 5.1 **The negotiating machinery**

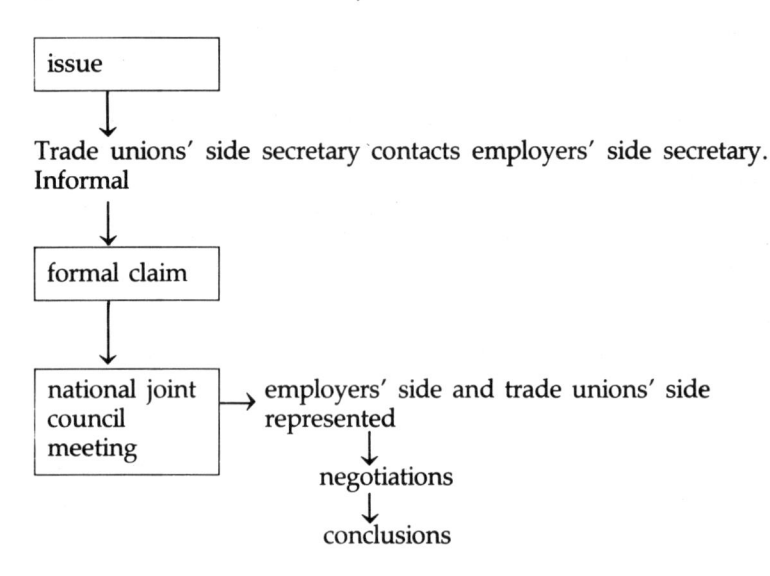

```
issue
  ↓
Trade unions' side secretary contacts employers' side secretary.
Informal
  ↓
formal claim
  ↓
national joint    →  employers' side and trade unions' side
council              represented
meeting                ↓
                     negotiations
                       ↓
                     conclusions
```

Fig. 5.2 The process

The second tier, the provincial level of negotiating machinery, is best represented by the Greater London Employers Secretariat, which carries out this function for the London area. It functions as an employers' secretariat at the provincial level, and can refer disputes and disagreements upwards to the national level.

The third tier, or local level, consists of joint committees composed of council Members and staff/worker representatives. For APT & C grades, common issues are raised, debated and resolved at this level if possible. They can of course also be referred upwards to the provincial level. The same principle is applied to manual workers, building trade operatives and craftspeople, where issues are raised, discussed and, if possible, resolved, at a joint works committee. This again includes elected Members and worker representatives. Councils determine the constitution, membership and organization of these joint committees. They are complex and vary from place to place.

In general, these committees meet as part of the committee cycle, with officers advising on specific issues and unions producing claims or problems for particular difficulties, such as overtime conditions and pay, or health and safety at work. There may also be specific committees which are concerned with single issues, such as job descriptions. Sexism and sexual harassment are also examples of specific issues. Industrial relations and personnel experts are often involved. These procedural events are part of and ratify the wider committee cycle, which is responsible for policy decisions at local level. This too has of course to be responsible to changing ideologies and pressures.

This formal machinery is controlled and organized, but 'local' issues are dealt with as and when they arrive – they may relate to particular problem areas, such as the contesting of job-evaluation decisions. However, 'presenting problems' are, as always, often not the 'real' issue, and can disguise other personnel issues, such as motivation, career problems or complex personal issues. They can also be used unconsciously as a way of perpetuating conflict and projecting anger or guilt from the self into other areas of the workplace. The resolution of local issues without taking the long-term effects of such reductions and decisions into consideration can also cause problems.

Presenting problems can also relate to power and the location of power. For example, workers involved in areas which are thought of as crucial are well aware of their bargaining power. This may be greatly in excess of any power which is thought to be wielded by information workers, for example. The use and manipulation of such awareness involves an understanding of current political and economic strategies and of ways of utilizing and exploiting these. Individuals or groups or committees may be involved in such manipulation, which produces complex effects on other groups, and diverts attention from service delivery. This manipulation is another example of power struggles, representing basic individual drives, affecting the workplace.

In education the Burnham machinery for teachers, (including library and information workers who may be employed on Burnham conditions), was dissolved, so that local agreements could be implemented in relation to national guidelines. A new pay-negotiating machinery has been established in its place. Again, there will be complex results, as without the machinery for free collective bargaining, opting out and local initiatives may produce a range of pay and conditions. These may be driven by market forces, comparability with other workers, or eventually be linked to competitive tendering.

In the university sector the Association of University Teachers is the recognized negotiating body, with local and national committees. The National Association of Teachers in Further and Higher Education is concerned with salaries and conditions of work in further and higher education. These are enshrined in the *Silver book*, but are being debated at local levels in some institutions of higher education. This is causing some difficulties.

These conditions are also recognized by the new Polytechnic Central Funding Council, currently involved in negotiating new conditions of service for all those previously employed on Burnham conditions of service. This follows the severance of the polytechnics from local-authority funding on 1 April 1989. Disputes over the implementation of new conditions of service rest on the need for nationally determined, not locally imposed, conditions. Polytechics now function as autonomous institutions and many are working out their own individual strategies and conditions of service.

The situation, however, is changing as the political climate alters. Industrial unrest in the 1960s and 1970s tended to be in manufacturing or transport, with collective bargaining procedures acting as a ceiling on pay claims, backed up by political initiatives. These then shifted to the public sector, as it was felt that this should be controlled in terms of pay claims linked to the concept of comparability. This was not well received by all the unions concerned. It was in contrast to the private sector, where market forces acted as the controlling factor. The idea that market forces and indicators rather than standardized agreements should determine pay and conditions did not make local conditions particularly stable and relaxed.

In the early 1980s this determination by market forces provided the theoretical base for a reconsideration of existing machinery. It also edited the changing social norms and values, and perceptions of local authorities and the 'public good'. The concept of smaller and locally accountable units then added to the way in which unions were seen to operate within this machinery, and there was a strong involvement towards a reduction in the power balance, with less input from trade unions, less obvious central control, and more local response. An example of local negotiating over conditions of service in the context of these political and social shifts can be seen in the case study of the London Borough of Wandsworth (Section 14). This encapsulates all the points mentioned above, and the move from national to local initiatives.

Local authorities, as the major public-sector employers (including education under this umbrella), of library and information workers, have in past years sometimes responded over and above conditions of service as laid down in national agreements, which may produce some difficulties in relation to performance-related pay. This is not only a resource issue, but a management issue also, as factors of measurement can also produce tensions between national norms and ideas, and local ideas. For example, the OAL concept of performance indicators in libraries, a national measurement, may not link with those being worked out locally. Performance measures in rural Northumbria or inner-city Lambeth have very little in common. They may, alternatively, have many qualitative factors in common, such as community involvement, not part of centrally produced quantitative factors. To add to the difficulties, performance-related pay is usually related to individual output or performance, rose-beds pruned or reference queries answered. At this individual level it also enhances the idea of very localized initiatives, and so freedom from a restrictive framework.

Job-description and job-evaluation processes are also affected, as these may vary from place to place or be part of a 'core' job description. Again, there may be difficulties in resolving differences between national and local ideas. In some places the concept of job evaluation and job descriptions is seen as prescriptive, and not as supporting market drives and changes. The appeals by those in the nursing profession against pay determined by job-evaluation processes illustrates the difficulties of implementing national schemes with local variations. Union representation and activities at local levels are also related to job descriptions and conditions of work.

Contract competitive tendering will also affect the framework, and will affect pay and conditions. Contract compliance is no longer a valid option. Conditions of service were placed outside the negotiating machinery. Local authorities are not able to tender using traditional 'conditions of pay' and so cannot necessarily compete economically with the private sector. Again, this is illustrated in Wandsworth, where companies will provide services to the local authority which has employees working to an entirely different set of conditions. Relationships at organizational and individual level will change accordingly. There will doubtless be a spill-over in terms of philosophy. The idea of service delivery at a local level is then provided by external or market forces, rather than by local authorities. The idea of service orientation then becomes an integral part of the private sector, so radically altering existing relationships.

Restrictive 'professional' ideas may also be seen as difficult, and so there may be moves to radicalize or 'free' training and education. This may lead to market forces and conditions of service driving job vacancies and also job retention. Local financial management for schools and colleges as well as current funding arrangements for the polytechnics may well add impetus to these ideas, in the context of a market economy. Traditional negotiating and job-evaluation procedures will then slowly disappear. Political polarization will also increase. Employee relationships may well become less stable.

The work of industrial tribunals will also affect employer/employee relationships. These tribunals operate at a national level and have statutory powers to deal with cases of discrimination, unfair dismissal, pay and other employment areas. An individual can take a case to a tribunal when he or she feels that he or she has been treated unfavourably, and when there is no collective agreement existing. The system is national, but is felt in some cases not to be able to react speedily enough, and may be reconsidered in relation to the role and structure of tribunals as a whole.

Managers need to understand the structures and processes, and be able to apply collective agreements with sensitivity in the workplace. They must also be able to understand the legislation and the way that it links with this process. The infrastructure of the organization must be adequate. Recognition of unions, involving time, training and attitudes, needs to be part of this structure and also involve all personnel. To complement this, managers must ensure that committees or departments are suitably structured and that communication lines are clear and logical. Joint negotiating committees are an example of support machinery. Personnel procedures must also recognize the conditions under which people are employed, and allow grievances and disciplinary issues to be handled appropriately. Legislation will also affect the implementation of conditions of work, including health and safety issues, as well as those covered by pay and conditions of work. Effective organization at a local level can help resolve many disputes which, if taken away from the local arena, can be not at all straightforward to resolve. The culture of the organization and corporate policies will help determine relationships.

References

1 National Joint Council for Local Authorities Administrative, Professional, Technical and Clerical Services, *Scheme of conditions of service*, London, NJCLA, 1975 (*Purple book*; updated each year. Also contains details of pay and conditions of service, job evaluation, training, car allowances, sick leave, etc.).
2 Greater London Joint Council for Local Authority Services (Manual Workers), *Schedule of wages and working conditions, and conditions, functions and recommendations of the council*, London, GLJCLAS, 1977 (*Buff book*; updated each year).
3 Greater London Joint Council for Craft and Trades Workers, *Handbook*, 4th ed., London GLJCCTW 1986 (*Green book*) (updated each year).

The working environment – contexts and issues 31

Further reading

Local Authorities Conditions of Service Advisory Board, *Pay, conditions of service and industrial relations in local government: an employers' strategy*, London, LACSAB, 1987.

National Joint Council for Further Education Lecturers in England and Wales, *Silver book*, rev. ed., London, NJCFE, 1987 (updated each year).

National Joint Council for Local Authority Services (Manual Workers), *Handbook*, rev. ed. , London, NJCLAS, 1988 (*White book*; contains details of wages, grading, structures, working arrangements, special provision, overtime, seasonal workers, bonus schemes, trainees, etc.).

Manager's notes

Distinguish between national, provincial and local levels of negotiations
Check the local negotiating structures
Relate these to the organization
Ensure the information (codes, etc.) is available and understood by everyone involved
Check that the legislation is also available
Disseminate information as and when appropriate
Use the structures and procedures sensitively

6 The negotiating process

The negotiating process operates through a series of identifiable processes, requiring specific skills and strategies, all of which interlink with personnel and industrial relations in general. The processes are an integral part of the negotiating machinery and operate within the culture, aims and objectives of the organization. Information will support and relate to these factors.

A clearly defined and basic area is that of the actual skills involved. These skills need to be acquired or developed by anyone involved in the negotiating process. This covers a wide range of situations, contexts and needs, from the very formal to the very casual and informal situation. It also involves personal feelings as well as unconscious and conscious drives, and so an understanding of the psychodynamic processes underlying individual and organizational behaviour is helpful. This understanding can be supported by clear communication methods and a knowledge of group and inter- and intra-group relationships. Signals can then be clearly interpreted.

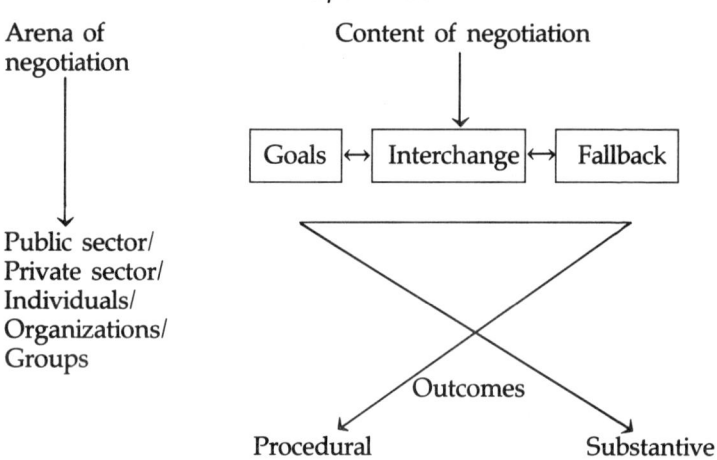

```
Arena of              Content of negotiation
negotiation
    |                         |
    |                         v
    |              ┌───────┐ ┌────────────┐ ┌──────────┐
    |              │ Goals │↔│ Interchange│↔│ Fallback │
    |              └───────┘ └────────────┘ └──────────┘
    v                    \                    /
Public sector/            \                  /
Private sector/            \                /
Individuals/                \              /
Organizations/               \   Outcomes /
Groups                        \  /      \/
                               \/       /\
                               /\      /  \
                              /  \    /    \
                         Procedural        Substantive
```

Fig. 6.1 Negotiating process

The skills flow from establishing *what* needs to be done (the end objective), into *how* it is done (presentation etc.), *when* and *where* the negotiating is carried out (the place and the climate), and with *whom* (ensuring that all those concerned are involved at the same level). It is first of all important, within the appropriate context, to establish the end objectives of the process: what is the required outcome? Second, it is important to establish if there are any fallback situations. Negotiating also involves establishing if the situation is 'all or nothing' or if compromises can be reached. The strategies to be used can then be planned in relation to the objectives, and the strategies of the 'other parties' worked out as far as possible. Compromise or confrontation may or may not be suitable but generally speaking 'strong' strategies and behaviour should not be used without careful planning.

Establishing a micro-framework for negotiating is the next step in the process. This involves clarifying procedures, setting the scene and establishing some kind of relationship with the person or people involved. This may be formal, including introductions and a statement on the actual situation, or informal, using first names and casual and friendly comments on the location. These relationships must fit with the socio-economic and political circumstances, and depend on sensitivity and initiative. The body language used during the preliminary scene-setting stage is important, and the physical setting – chairs, tables and desks – is crucial. A confrontational climate is quickly established, but is equally quickly broken down.

The working environment – contexts and issues

The organizational attitude to negotiating procedures is important and reflects individual attitudes.

Once the climate has been determined, then the short and long-term objectives of the specific meeting, negotiating process or bargaining have to be established. This is done in relation to time available, which sets the pace, and the information which has been circulated, as well as the overt and covert objectives of all those involved. Some kind of statement which sets parameters and helps define a way forward is a very helpful element in defining the purpose of the meeting. This analysis and overview prevents a 'hidden agenda' from developing and hindering the stated and circulated agenda.

This leads into defining clearly what are the expected or hoped-for outcomes of the process – in other words, what actual objectives, outcomes or agreements need to be finalized. The outcomes will probably be either *procedural* (affecting grievances, which often lead to changes in the negotiating machinery) or *substantive* (relating to conditions of work, and especially wages). Bargaining on matters concerned with pay tends to be collectively labelled as 'distributive' bargaining and that concerned with discipline and general matters as 'integrative'. In both cases it is possible to work out the costs, both real and personal, in relation to the desired outcomes. This has to be approached carefully and information used must link to climate and context. It relates also to the information which is available and which has been circulated. Efficient information also helps reduce confusion and ambiguity and ensures that the framework of negotiation will provide support. (Codes of practice are also frameworks.)

Individuals, or parties, can then move into the core of the situation, which is exchanging, discussing and agreeing, or not, on the information. Agendas must be set and agreed, and, as indicated earlier, these also set the climate, as well as indicating pressures and conflicts. (The formal agenda will of course disguise informal issues.) Language is a crucial clue to formal and informal meanings and complements body language. Eye contact, attitudes, facial expressions and aggressive responses are all part of the informal responses which can support or detract from the process. The agenda is the beginning of the formal negotiating process. At this stage, it is important not to be side-tracked by unimportant elements, and to maintain a clear overview of the whole proceedings.

At this stage of the negotiating process, pace and style are important and again relate to climate and context. It is not helpful to work at a pace which is not in step with other people or parties, or in a style which is radically different. If this happens, then tensions will arise which will prevent progress towards an idea or possible settlement or agreement. It is also helpful to try and work out why styles differ so radically, so that personal presenting characteristics do not determine the agenda. Clear definitions of intent need to be established, so that each side of the negotiating table understands the perceptions and aims of the other. Sensitivity to signals is essential. Listening skills are vital.

The agenda, which symbolizes the central issue of the situation, is linked to the messages and images presented by the information. The ultimate objective may be part of the financial-planning process, including performance reviews, for example, or establishing new job descriptions, or settling a claim for overtime, to name but a few. The tone and use of words in the setting out of the information is also a contributory factor to effective negotiation. The main arguments must be clearly established. Those involved must have clearly laid-out, supportive information available to them, have been briefed on it and clearly understand all the ramifications. Opening situations are crucial. Failure to carry out any of these elements as far as information is concerned inevitably leads to confusion and disarray. Situations will determine the information handling to some extent, but this rather resembles a game of cards. The introductory information and opening discussions will set the scene, but not disclose all the needs and wants of the card holder, and more will be disclosed as the meeting unfolds. Each crucial piece of information is another card to be played – if the aces are discarded first, the subsequent needs can easily be trumped. Positions will change from day to day and from power to weakness and back again. The concept also helps in the control and organization of information. It also helps establish the arguments and strengths of the other person or people involved.

Timing is another element which has to be managed. This too depends on sensitivity and initiative. There may be a need to break off negotiations and resume them later, but such breaks or adjustments must be handled with care. Poor handling will confuse secondary and primary issues and so the total negotiating process. Or there may be an opportunity to proceed in a very informal way. The parameters need to be flexible but also need to be maintained. Flexibility is not the same as chaos.

The finalizing of the process is part of the timing. The actual finalizing procedures will vary from the commercial to the public sector, but the finalizing summarizes issues of agreement and points the way forward for action. It may involve giving out considerable amounts of information, or outlining areas for future discussion. Industrial and commercial agreements tend to be complex and lengthy. The timing of the summarizing is important, as other agreements and situations can be influenced by this. The style and handling of the final agreement also enhances the credibility of those involved. This part of the process is also important in finalizing interim agreements or clarifying sticking points. These must have been clearly established in the mind and plan of the negotiator in the first place, and are part of the control of information.

Many of the skills described in the section on counselling support are also important, such as observing, participating, listening, reflecting, communicating, advocating, interpreting and summarizing. These may be verbal or non-verbal. The use of language and the linking of behaviour to body language will, of course, depend all the way through on those involved and the anticipated and needed outcome. Language in negotiating is very important, and the precise words used indicate the underlying meaning. For example, for a negotiator to state 'that is the absolute limit of my offer' means just that — there can be no further discussion. To state 'that is probably the general limit of my offer' means that the negotiator is unsure of his or her ground, and that there is plenty of room for manoeuvring, both in power terms and in actual outcomes. Careful listening is again important, as well as necessary. Again card playing is a good analogy. Humour is an element that can be used in this — but requires sensitivity and tact from the negotiators.

The skills involved throughout the process will also relate to the context and culture of the organization and to the credibility and perceived power (and sometimes status) of those involved in the organization. Issues such as managerial styles, alliances, equal opportunities policies, race and gender struggles will help determine language and skills. At the same time these can also reflect strong personal desires and ambiguities, and so the 'apparent' negotiating stance may be the outward manifestation of inward need. The awareness of this depends on an individual's perception and knowledge of him or herself. The skilled negotiator will achieve more, partly through an understanding of the individual and group psychodynamic processes. The machinery and organizational structure may, and probably will, be used as a mechanism for the conscious or unconscious drives of the participants. This understanding of the self then helps those involved in negotiating to adopt suitable styles and stances, and to work with others in the situation to focus on the *real* and pre-determined issues, rather than on issues of power assertion and rewards. Power, of course, may be personal power, or power stemming from the institution or organization or from external agencies, but it has a strong effect in deciding how and when and where skills are used. Competence and preparation are the important power elements in this context (see also Section 8).

The negotiating process must also be seen in the context of the size, status and perceived power of the union or unions involved, and the industrial relations policies of the organization. Procedures, training, skills, attitudes, structures and perceptions will vary in relation to the context. Knowledge of the legislation is another crucial strand. The process of negotiating will also formally involve a range of people whose roles, relationships and stances must be understood by all those involved. The balance of these relationships is a crucial factor.

The two major groups involved in the process are:

Management. The term is used as a collective for any member of an organization seen to hold a position of power or authority and involved in the negotiating process. This power may be real or imagined, and can apply to a collection of people, one person, or a person with a remit for industrial relations negotiating. This is frequently the personnel department, with responsibility held by a senior member of staff. Organizations will have their own negotiating processes and hierarchies, with representatives assigned or elected to the task, and with titles and rewards appropriate to the culture of the organization. The communication process and information-handling process will also be influenced by context and culture. Management will in turn be represented by unions, varying in relation to organization and activity, but in any negotiating process, these representatives of management are clearly 'union' and not 'management'. The role, title, structure and information handling of a union representing management are crucial, as group and individual boundaries can easily become blurred and confused.

Union, perceived as a 'catch all' phrase for anyone with a union involvement in the negotiating process. The union element is thus the other side of the management/managed relationship. The union can be represented in a variety of informal and formal ways, representing those who are managed. This representation can be informal and established as a result of organization relationships, or formal within the negotiating process. Informal representation includes pre-meeting discussions, circulation of information, scheduled but unminuted meetings, and 'casual' lunch and coffee meetings. Formal representation is achieved through scheduled meetings, with a structure and minutes, or through the official negotiating machinery, by recognized union representatives. These representatives can be shop stewards, workplace stewards, branch secretaries, regional secretaries and others appointed by election. Each union, white-collar, blue-collar, manual or other title, has a clear set of procedures for electing representatives, an established negotiating hierarchy and recognized titles for each post. As in the management arena, titles, positions and structure will vary in relation to size, geographical location, character of the industry or occupation, and be appropriate to the culture and ethos of the union. The ethos of union representation has been influenced by strong social forces, which have produced this range of regional and occupational differences.

The current situation may well become much more complex as the legislation changes, and as political and economic forces alter the negotiating tensions. Changes in the concept of the 'closed shop' will affect the process of recruitment and the climate in which a union operates. These are linked to the concept of collective bargaining, which involves both management and unions in a process which results in some outcome affecting behaviour or conditions of work. The agreement which emerges as a result of such negotiations is then held by both sides.

The tactics and strategies evolved and utilized by both sides form another element, related to the procedures and machinery involved. These tactics include the familiar ones of working to rule, working in specific areas only, disregarding elements of job descriptions, strike action, withdrawal of good will, limited withdrawal of labour, overtime bans, refusal to carry out crucial elements of a job (e.g. marking exam papers) and a host of others. These range from all-pervasive industrial action to modified action. Such strategies and tactics are employed by managers and managed and will reflect specific situations and cultures. These varied tactics are resolved in relation to the conditions and ethos of the place of employment. They may be handled and resolved informally or formally, using disciplinary or other procedures. These in turn are part of the negotiating machinery. The way in which they are handled forms part of the negotiating process.

Disciplinary and grievance procedures have clearly established rules and applications and must be fully understood by employers and employees. How and why they are implemented, in relation to specific instances such as dismissal, are clearly laid down. These rules are contained in the appropriate agreements, such as the *Buff book* and the *Purple book* discussed earlier, and designed to achieve the resolution of conflicts through agreed decisions.

Yet again, a current example of change is the new conditions of service for teaching staff which are being implemented in the polytechnics following their move away from local-authority funding and conditions of service, and in schools as a result of LMS. The negotiating process needs clearly defined outcomes and requires members of the appropriate unions to be equally well informed and involved as management. Conflict resolution is difficult in situations where the context is rapidly changing, and illustrates the need for frameworks. The situation also clearly illustrates the effects of political and economic change on conditions of work and the negotiating processes. Local agreements which are emerging as a result of these changes will further complicate, weaken or destroy the national negotiating framework and national consensus.

It is important that staff are trained in the art of negotiating, in relation to their role in the organization. This will also depend on the size of the structure and the availability of departments or specialists involved in this work. Communication skills, time management, role playing and information and documentation presentation are all important elements. An understanding of procedures, including timing and the general management of meetings is also important. These can all be included in in-house training programmes, but are skills that develop with constant use. An understanding of the psychodynamics of power initiatives and group behaviour is important. This is part of the wider skills of analysis and synthesis, essential to those involved in negotiating.

Further reading
ACAS, *An industrial relations handbook*, London, ACAS, 1980.
Cosmo, G. and Lewis, N., *The role of ACAS conciliation in equal pay and sex discrimination cases*, Manchester, Equal Opportunities Commission, 1985.
Industrial relations in Britain: an Industrial Relations Services guide, London, Industrial Relations Services, 1988.
Kennedy, G., Benson, J. and Macmillan, J., *Managing negotiations*, 2nd ed., London, Business Books, 1984.
Thomson, G., *Textbook of industrial relations management*, London, Institute of Personnel Management, 1984.
Todd, K., 'Collective bargaining and professional associations in the library field', *Library quarterly*, 55 (3), 1985, 284–99.

Manager's notes

Analyse the required outcome for disputes and difficulties
Establish what negotiating needs to be done
Determine objectives and strategies
Establish how negotiations are to be carried out (process)
Decide when negotiations take place and with whom (task)
Check where they take place

Involve all the appropriate people
Disseminate information
Finalize strategies
Meet
Eventually, finalize outcome(s) – procedural or substantive

7 Counselling support

Anyone involved in personal relationships in the work context becomes involved in counselling support at some point and at some level. This may take the form of brief and temporary concern with a colleague's personal problems, or involve long-term counselling related to a specific problem or issue. It may also involve friendship or temporary support. Counselling may be formalized, that is offered by a trained counsellor, or may be semi- or part-formalized, that is offered by a person as a part of his or her managerial or supervisory role. The range of support offered is also reflected in the range of expertise and training available. These in turn reflect changes in organizational styles, expectations of work, changing lifestyles and the growing 'investment' in human resources by organizations. This may or may not be altruistic and can also be linked to the changes outlined in the Introduction. Such changes are also part of a recognition by managers that a healthy organization is more effective in terms of relationships and outputs, and so investment in human resources is realistic. Counselling relates to the issues of social and political concern outlined earlier, as these affect organizations and so relationships within these organizations.

At a personal level, the complexities which derive from social and economic pressures need to be recognized in the work situation. It is important to maintain balance between a range of demands in order to achieve both at home and at work, and the skills involved in counselling can sometimes help to achieve this balance. The psychodynamic drives which contribute to the balance or imbalance need to be understood if serious consideration of particular personal issues is undertaken. The 'presenting' issue or area of contention in the work situation can be a reflection of earlier inadequate support, or the manifestation of unconscious drives and projections. These have to be related to behavioural patterns for individuals and groups if any meaningful change is to be developed. The importance of the person underlines the person-centred, non-judgemental and non-directive aspects of counselling. If the growth of the *individual* is at the core of such support, then the non-directive aspects are crucial. Other motives are highly suspect! The underlying dynamics are especially important in the context of disputes and of management and union relationships.

Counselling is an important part of this human resource investment, especially if fully integrated into the organizational structure and culture. It is as relevant to a library and information service as to a large multi-national firm. Counselling can encompass a range of situations including not only the effects of industrial relations, but issues of race and gender, redundancy, relationships and bereavement.

Although, as mentioned earlier, the term 'counselling' covers a range of activities and represents different aspects of personal relations to different people, it is possible to quote one widely accepted definition, from the British Association for Counselling. This definition can then help define the skills needed, and so the situations where such skills can be helpful:

> People become engaged in counselling when a person occupying regularly or temporarily the role of counsellor offers or agrees explicitly to offer time, attention and respect to another person or persons temporarily in the role of client.
>
> The task of counselling is to give the client an opportunity to explore, discover and clarify ways of living more resourcefully and toward greater well-being.

In the organizational situation, it may be necessary to clearly define counselling in relation to generalized support, so that those involved are not caught up in confusions arising from blurred boundaries. A formal counselling service is easily recognizable and recognized, even with a variety of names, but other situations are less clear. If boundaries are not clear, then expectations on either side become uncertain and so communication becomes confused and acrimonious. Responsibilities on both sides in assessment situations, for example, involve a maturity of approach and a clear understanding of boundaries. Counselling may even follow or be suggested as a result of assessment procedures, but it is not part of the process. Successfully integrated, it will be a crucial element in personal development.

The skills involved in counselling can be identified, although they do of course overlap and inter-relate with other skills needed in interpersonal relationships. Two of the most important ones to be distinguished are those of listening and observing. Listening is an active process and requires care, concentration and attention, rather than a sponge-like absorption. Body language, supportive responses and tone all indicate interest and concentration. Observing involves working with another person while watching for physical evidence of unease, stress, distress or other signals of discomfort. Body

The working environment – contexts and issues

language, verbal clues, movement, eye movement and so on are all clues to relationships and states of anxiety or need. Reflecting is important, involving interpreting and feeding back signals in the one-to-one situation, while at the same time analysing the interaction between counsellor and client, or manager and managed, or teacher and student. Diagnosing and analysing issues is crucial. So is communicating – talking is rarely considered to be a skill but in true communication it forms a vital part. Diagnosing hidden agendas in relation to 'presenting issues' is an important skill, while empathy, intuition and the awareness of when to refer to other agencies is important. Counselling also involves developing other skills, such as empathy, and an awareness of the importance of individual choice and individual attitudes. Counselling can be seen as developing these skills to produce a helping non-directive situation, in which a person can explore and begin to resolve his/her own problems.

Referral is important in relation to the clarification of boundaries, so that counselling does not become confused with other activities. It can be categorized as an active or a 'doing' process. As a result of assessment procedures, union disputes or demarcation disputes, it may be a necessary process. Referral provides support, using other appropriate agencies, either inside or outside the organization. There may be a need for further training, for example, to support the tasks involved in a new job description. There may be a need for the counsellor (or counsellor/manager) to suggest referral to other specialized agencies. These can include redundancy or retirement counselling, careers guidance, specific information and support for women, older employees, minority groups, or those who need to communicate more assertively. Racism and sexism are two areas where specific needs may have to be addressed.

All of these can be grouped together as *directive* elements, and so can be distinguished from the counselling element, which is essentially *non-directive*. These differences clarify the role of the counsellor, and his or her perceived role in the management structure, and the style and ethos of the organization.

In the library and information service context, counselling should and will be integrated into the system in a way that is appropriate to local circumstances. This may include a formal counselling section, or the enhancement of management skills to include those of counselling activities which may spill over into other areas of personal relationships, such as career counselling, re-entry into education, research activities and, of course, the assessment and training areas. One person may take on different roles at different times, and so there is a need for the boundaries to be maintained.

The whole area of counselling is growing rapidly, and its importance may underline the tensions and confusions which exist in many individuals. Current changes, such as performance related pay add to these fears.

Counselling is a structured process and provides a base for identifying or clarifying a problem or issue which is of concern to an individual. The process involves a range of skills and the goals will vary from situation to situation. It is important that the organization is clear about the value it places on counselling, so that managers can integrate the process into their planning. There is a need to evaluate counselling, and some of these issues link with library and information service dilemmas. Performance indicators in the area of counselling have many elements common to all the caring and service professions, and are relevant to their implementation in the library and information profession.

Personal awareness will enhance the understanding of a manager about him or herself and contribute to an awareness of the needs of individuals and groups within an organization. It is essential to good counselling practice. Counselling helps provide satisfying work conditions, prevents rapid staff turnover, and supports institutional and personal objectives.

Further reading
Bion, W. R., *Experiences in groups*, London, Tavistock, 1961.
Bion, W. R., *Learning from experience*, London, Heinemann, 1962.
De Board, R., *Counselling people at work: an introductory guide for managers*, London, Gower, 1983.
Lyth, I. M., *Containing anxiety in institutions*, London, Free Association Books, 1988.
Milne, A. R., *Counselling at work*, Bromley, Centre for Professional Employment Counselling, 1988 (Occasional papers No. 2).
Reddy, M., *The manager's guide to counselling at work*, London, Methuen, 1987.
Richardson, E., *The teacher, the school and the task of management*, London, Heinemann Educational, 1973.
Salzberger-Wittenberg, I., *Psycho-analytic insight and relationships*, London, Routledge and Kegan Paul, 1970.
Storr, A., *The art of psychotherapy*, London, Secker and Warburg, 1979.

Manager's notes
Differentiate between counselling, advice, advocacy and referral
Ensure that the organization understands the value of counselling

Interpret philosophy into policies and practices
Identify skills (those existing and those needed)
Provide training
Honour confidentiality
Honour the definition of counselling

8 Psychodynamic aspects of industrial relations Rossana Kendall

This section tries to describe a framework for understanding industrial relations which is based on Isabel Menzies'[1] application to organizations[1] of the analytical work of Melanie Klein.[2] The level of understanding this model offers can generate a fresh set of alternatives for managers attempting to handle industrial relations problems. An effort is made to apply this model to industrial relations in library and information systems, and then to outline some of the insights this offers and some alternative approaches to industrial relations which suggest themselves as a result. One of these approaches is based on the work of the psychiatrist, D. W. Winnicott.[3] Klein's theories appear at first to be dense and possibly irrelevant, but can illuminate some organizational issues. Menzies developed and demonstrated their relevance to managers in her work on social systems.

Klein suggested that the mechanisms an infant uses to defend itself against severe anxiety up to the age of five months involve the infant's splitting off its sense of its own badness, projecting this badness, and then feeling persecuted by the object onto which the badness has been projected. This way of coping Klein called the paranoid/schizoid position. The baby, in pain because hungry, feels that it is bad; it denies its badness, splits it off, and projects it onto a bad mother. At the same time it has a phantasy that there is an ideally good mother. Having projected its bad feelings onto mother, it then feels persecuted by them in the form of mother. The splitting of good and bad gives the term 'schizoid', and the feeling of being persecuted gives 'paranoid'. Menzies showed how these mechanisms can be used by a whole organization through a process of unconscious collusion between its members, to attempt to deal with a high level of anxiety.[4]

Klein also suggested that, at about the age of five months, the infant becomes aware that the bad, persecuting object is also the mother whom it loves. It can no longer keep up the imagined split between the two imagined mothers. It fears the damage it may have done to the object it loves – the mother – and feels guilt and concern at the destruction it has wrought. This damage has been done in unconscious phantasy but at this stage the infant has no sense of the difference between its feelings and phantasies and their effects in the real world, so it imagines that what it has phantasized (damage to the mother) has been done. It feels depression, guilt, concern, sadness and grief, as well as having to handle the ambivalence of being aware that it both hates and loves the same person. Out of healthy guilt and concern it wishes to make acts of reparation towards the mother, to make up for the imagined damage it has done. If the mother can acknowledge these overtures and can contain the infant's anxiety at its guilt, the infant acquires a sense of its own creativity, ability to make amends and to be loved. It can tolerate the ambivalence of its feelings and feel some reciprocity in exchanges between itself and the environment. Klein called this the depressive position.

Without using the term 'depressive position', Menzies suggests ways of moving towards defence mechanisms which are more creative than the paranoid/schizoid: these are to do with the working through of anxiety and the creativity associated with the depressive position.[5]

It would seem that the union-versus-management split, where each side sees the other as dreadful and itself as righteous, is an organizational defence against anxiety. It is as if the organization is like the infant, and splits what it perceives, imagining one part to be ideally good and the other very, very bad. This is the paranoid/schizoid defence mechanism used by a group of people instead of an individual. It occurs when the organization experiences high levels of anxiety, and some situations in which this might happen are examined below.

Anxiety grows when staff are not well looked after, or not well managed. The staff group of a library and information system provides a service to the client group. The quality of the service to the client is inextricably linked to, and depends on, the well-being of the staff; it is linked to the quality of 'service' the staff receives in terms of effective management. Successful organizations, then, tend to be those which care for their staff and demonstrate this care in a variety of ways: conditions of service, medical schemes, pension schemes, car leasing, training, perks, etc. A management which insists that staff focus on service to the client without, in turn, making sure that the staff group is well looked after, is likely to see levels of staff anxiety rising and to be heading for trouble with the unions. Since library and information systems are very much services, it is important for managers to bear in mind the need to balance service considerations with staff welfare, in order for the organization to be successful in its primary task of service provision – there is a pragmatic motivation as well as a moral duty to look after staff.

Many situations which arouse anxiety are usually grouped loosely under the term 'change'. This may be, to name some examples, a change in technologies, tasks, staff, staffing structure, clientele, ideology, resources, buildings or management. Such changes may hold excitement as well as a degree of anxiety for some; these are often the people who conceived the changes and therefore feel powerful and competent in the evolving situation. The acute anxiety produced by such situations is most often experienced by those who do *not* feel powerful, who are not the initiators but have, rather, a reactive role and thus feel incompetent and de-skilled: the change was not fashioned to match *their* skills and visions. It is important for managers to be aware that even the smallest change may arouse apparently irrational levels of anxiety in their staff. At times of change, staff may feel their identity and competence to be at risk. Training staff to understand and manage change is a useful strategy.

Perhaps management has traditionally overlooked its responsibility for staff welfare; perhaps it is appropriate that staff should not be dependent on management, but should unite to safeguard its own well-being. Whatever their origins, the function of unions is to ensure the well-being of bodies of workers. But the responsibility for staff well-being should be shared – not split – between union and management; each should acknowledge the importance of staff well-being towards fulfilment of the primary task. However, the symmetrical structure created by having two 'ruling' bodies (union and management) provides a scenario which is ripe for splitting and, where there is stress in an organization, union and management may move apart. It may look as if the union is not interested in the task, or as if management is not interested in the staff; it may seem to the union that *it* is good and management diabolical, while to management it may seem that *it* is good and the union diabolical. Thus at times both find it difficult to share responsibility for improving conditions of work for staff – something which it is in both their interests to do.

A good tactic could be for senior management to move negotiations with unions down the hierarchical line, so that the negotiating parties are contiguous in the hierarchy and there is less symbolic distance between the parties seeking to find common ground.

Many organizations seem to make extensive use of other paranoid/schizoid defence mechanisms which Menzies noted in the group of hospitals she wrote about. These were the splitting of the task and of relationships, and denial of the individual, which latter was expressed in a number of ways, a major one being denial of responsibility. This in turn led to avoidance of decisions, as well as the polarities of negative projection and idealization. Additionally there was denial of feelings and of relationships. This resulted in under-employment of staff in terms of level and amount of work, a sense of detachment from the job, which, however, also reduced job satisfaction, and the fact that mistakes were not acceptable. So the paranoid/schizoid defences, which 'inhibit the capacity for creative, symbolic thought'[6] result in the individual losing a sense of his or her ability to do a job effectively. It is ironic that change, which can create the high levels of anxiety which lead to paranoid/schizoid defence mechanisms, is then inhibited by these very mechanisms.

Most library and information systems exist within a hierarchy, which is a structure designed to split levels and there is a (sometimes acute) division between professional and so-called non-professional staff; then tasks and relations are often further split by rotas, which leads to different people working together and with the client group. This is fertile ground for the growth of a defence mechanism based on splitting. Reducing the divisions between professional and 'non-professional' staff, as well as varying rotas, might reduce the probability of splitting. It would also enhance communication, which is in itself a powerful way of preventing divisions and misunderstanding.

If goodness and badness are held to be possessed by different individuals and groups, then it is likely that splitting is taking place, the so-called good splitting off their so-called badness and projecting it onto some other individual or group. Any form of prejudiced discrimination is a clear example of various splitting and projecting mechanisms. Perhaps there is a function within a library and information service which is traditionally considered to be 'bad', or it might be the staff in a particular geographical area or building. The statement: 'Oh, it's that awful lot in ... again. What can you expect? They'll never change!' may be a sign of splitting. And indeed it is not in the speaker's apparent interest for them to change, because that would mean the speaker re-owning some of the awfulness and thus changing too.

Sometimes attacks are made on members of staff by other individuals or groups, and the former are told not to take it personally, a denial of them as individuals, and of their feelings of hurt/anger. Demands for guidelines on almost every aspect of the service, combined with upward delegation, are an avoidance of decision-making and responsibility; taking responsibility for making a decision invites the projection of badness. Or, again, the past may be denied or record of it lost. There may be great emphasis on serving the public, on fulfilling the needs of all the clientele, and on removing all obstacles to its using the services, yet when some of that idealized clientele turn out to be abusive and violent or thieves, then security forces are brought in, or security systems introduced. This is a good example of the counterpoint of idealization and rigid control, a manifestation of paranoid/schizoid defence mechanisms.

Mistakes are, of course, unacceptable within such an environment: to make a mistake is to be 'bad'. But the especially unacceptable mistakes are those which contravene the defence systems: a suggestion, say, that responsibility might lie other than where the organization's collusive systems have placed it, or a suggestion that there might be a middle way, avoiding either side of a split.

Marris[7] has suggested that change, like bereavement, evokes feelings of loss and requires a working through of feelings of ambivalence. This ambivalence is about being torn between the past and the future; it gives rise to conflict within the individual or group. If this conflict becomes intolerable and cannot be held within, then it is externalized, and the individual or group takes up a position of conflict with another individual or group. Thus, following this line of reasoning, an organization undergoing change will feel ambivalent about the change and may externalize that conflict in a polarization between individuals or groups within the organization. This may produce what Marris calls an 'ideology of conflict'. Union and management may be two such groups, 'and their conflict may be the way towards working out the ambivalence produced by change and, as such, should not be suppressed but rather negotiated through to the end'. It is worth quoting Marris at length here because his ideas may explain resistances which seem incomprehensible (Marris uses the word 'grieving' because he relates the emotions felt during change to those felt at a bereavement).

> So when reforms create confusion in relationships, they are likely to be more manageable when they allow a structure of oppositions to evolve.
>
> This is a hard truth for reformers to accept, I think. To them, their proposals are already the resolution of a problem, which represents the public interest. The success of the changes seems to depend on goodwill and mutual understanding; conflict only frustrates the co-operation that will best serve everyone. But this attitude betrays the rationalism which makes any form of grieving unintelligible. If changes are disruptive, they do not become at once assimilable just because they may be good sense. The continuity of understanding has still to be restored, by testing what relationships now mean in terms which can be derived from what they used to mean.[8]

It could be suggested that unions are there to ensure that this latter happens, in the face of a drive for progress from a management which does not or cannot look to relationships, and that the negotiations of this pair provide the new meaning with which the organization can move forward.

This takes time – any change takes time. Managers have to come to terms with this fact. If time is not allowed initially, progress will almost inevitably be blocked at a later stage. Similarly, ambivalence has to be acknowledged, even if only privately; both managers and stewards will be feeling ambivalent about the change itself and about their roles: there are few stewards who do not want to be managers and few managers who do not remember being part of the 'lowerarchy'.

Menzies pointed out that the wastage caused by the defence systems in the hospital was essential; otherwise there would have been too many trained nurses available in comparison with the number of jobs.[9] Thus it could be said that the defence systems were a purposeful way of controlling the workforce. The same can apply in library and information services and the organizations to which they may belong: high levels of anxiety mean that staff make mistakes. Mistakes are often unacceptable; staff may be disciplined and dismissed for them. Other staff, finding the levels of anxiety intolerable, leave for other jobs. This can mean a very significant turnover in personnel, which actually suits the aim of those in control of the organization, that aim being to change the culture, and the most efficient way of achieving that aim being a change in type of personnel. In many organizations, the level of wastage of staff caused by the defence system is actually purposeful – though perhaps at an unconscious level.

There may be another, perhaps unconscious, level of purpose in a union/management dichotomy: such a situation means that it is difficult to progress change and new policies, and although unions and management may be ostensibly in conflict, at another level they may be united in not wanting to implement a policy, say, imposed on them by a third party. The stasis caused by their conflict enables both parties both to do nothing and also to avoid responsibility for doing nothing.

Are there constant crises because of staff shortages? Are there high levels of staff turnover, and of occasional sickness? Are buildings often shut down as staffing levels required are rigidly adhered to in these places? Are 'non-professional' staff under-employed and not developed? Do 'professional' staff have to do 'non-professional' work in order to keep the service going? Is there very little job satisfaction? Are staff who attempt not to collude with the splitting the very ones who are targeted with accusations of being 'bad' (an attempt to re-impose the split on them)? All of the above are signs of paranoid/schizoid defences in operation, most of them having been noted by Menzies in her hospitals.

Just as the infant has to move from the paranoid/schizoid to the depressive position in order to develop, so an organization has to find ways of doing the same. Someone or some function needs to hold the depressive position for the organization, and to move it towards working through depressive anxieties, partly so that change can be better effected in an integrated way. Perhaps managers can exercise leadership by doing this, by holding the middle ground, by refusing to collude with splits between good and bad.

So how can industrial relations become an opportunity for negotiating a way through conflict, as opposed to a problem which creates even more conflict? How can they start to become an enhancing part of organizational development rather than a blight? Partly by people starting to think of them in that way.

Perhaps the work of Winnicott, another analyst, can offer some ideas; he suggested that, to develop healthily, the infant needs a set of surroundings which nurture growth in the sense of psychological development: 'maturational processes require and depend on the facilitating environment'.[10] Part of this environment he called the area of play, or the transitional space. This is not external reality, nor is it simply the individual's inner world. It is a bridging place between the two, where the individual has the chance to engage in creative processes which form a personal negotiation between the two worlds.

In order to mature, to develop effectively in performing its primary task, an organization needs something to fulfil the function of the facilitating environment. Furthermore, staff within the organization need the organization itself to be a facilitating environment if they are to develop. This role may be fulfilled by an actual place: a staff room, for instance. Or else a function may do the trick: training, staff welfare, personnel, counselling services. Or, perhaps best of all, good management provides the key facilitating element in the environment. A training course is a very good example of an area of play, of illusion which is not the reality of the organization's primary task yet is closely related to it, providing course participants with an opportunity to explore how they will shape their individual contributions, which spring from their individual reality, to the primary task. A good supervisory session with a line manager also provides a transitional space, off the job but not away on a course, to review and think about work performance and strategy. A counselling facility, offered by management or a welfare officer or the personnel function, provides a similar transitional area. In these places staff can process their experience, trying to make sense of it in different ways. They can do the work of worrying; they can confront their anxieties, usually in their symbolic form (the work situation) rather than their original form (memories of infancy); they can formulate strategies for carrying on with the task in the face of extreme anxieties – or sometimes simply have had enough space away from the task to make it possible to return to the task. Most of all, staff can internalize the use of the transitional space, a commitment to giving themselves space to review process issues – a commitment to learning.

This issue of learning is a key point: if the organizational culture is a learning culture, events take on a different value. They are all clues to meaning, all opportunities for learning and developing. So, within a learning environment industrial relations are a useful indicator of crucial issues and a pointer towards new learning, instead of (or perhaps more realistically as well as) an irritation. Managers constantly review their responses to and management of industrial relations, learn about them and develop increasingly helpful ones.

Winnicott further postulated the existence of transitional phenomena within the area of play, which partake of the real/not real quality of that area, combining the ability both to contain the individual's anxieties and also to offer her/him the opportunity to address those anxieties in a flexible, experimental environment – to play and be creative. The archetypal transitional phenomenon is the teddy bear.

Individuals, functions, or objects (perhaps even something very humble) may fulfil the function of a transitional object, being the recipient of anxieties and in some cases offering a container within which they can be managed creatively. So if a teapot, or whether to have yellow or green labels, or some such apparently trivial item, takes up most of the discussion time of a staff meeting, that may be because these items have become a way for staff to express and manage their anxieties and are, as such, extremely important. For the same reason, it is important not to overlook the importance of any apparently small issues which a union raises.

To conclude: a library and information system's primary task is to deliver a service to the public. This is the primary task of all staff. Managers have an additional primary task, which is to manage resources, especially staff. An organization can be seen as having three levels, the top one to do with the task, the next down to do with the emotional needs of staff, and the third, and least accessible, to do with staff's unconscious impulses and anxieties. A manager's task encompasses all three levels. In other words, it is a manager's job to manage resources with the aim of fulfilling the organization's primary task. Staff are potentially the greatest resource an organization has; their performance is affected by all three levels of the organization; therefore a manager needs to be able to work, as far as possible, with all three levels: the individual and collective unconscious, staff's emotional needs, and the primary task. This means that the manager's primary task has a component which is additional to the organization's primary task and, although this component is subordinate to the primary task, it is also crucial to it. If the organizational culture is such that managers do not recognize the existence of emotions in and around them, these emotions do not just go away. They demand expression and space, and union activity is a way of allowing that space. The complexity of the situation is compounded by the fact that managers are caught up in their organization's dynamics, making it hard sometimes to maintain an objective focus. So one of the aims of management development work is to push the emotional and unconscious levels up into managers' primary task fields, and to develop a management able to acknowledge and handle that degree of complexity and subtlety. More than being able to use basic interpersonal skills, being able to speak the language of the unions, we are talking about a management able to design strategies for industrial relations, able to plan for outcomes, able to keep long-term aims in mind always, able to avoid a dichotomy between action and feeling, able to avoid emotional reactions and able to act out of an acknowledgement and understanding of emotion.

References
1 Menzies, I. E. P., *The functioning of social systems as a defence against anxiety*, London, Tavistock Institute of Human Relations, 1970.
2 See, for example, Klein, M., *Our adult world and other essays*, London, Heinemann, 1963.
3 See, for example, Winnicott, D. W., *The family and individual development*, London, Tavistock, 1965.
4 Menzies, op. cit.
5 Ibid., 25.
6 Ibid., 35.
7 Marris, P., *Loss and change*, London, Routledge and Kegan Paul, 1974.
8 Ibid., 98.
9 Menzies, op. cit., 22.

10 'Communicating and not communicating leading to a study of certain opposites', in Winnicott, D. W., *The maturational processes and the facilitating environment*, London, Hogarth Press, 1972.

Manager's notes

Consider the psychodynamic approach to i/r as an alternative or supportive approach
Relate some of the major theories to your organization
Try and identify some of the key issues which are causing tension
Relate to these in a non-confrontational way
Develop strategies to support personal growth in your organization
Facilitate training and development in this area

Part Two

Perspectives: viewpoints from practitioners, professionals and unions

Introduction to Part Two

Organizations involved in industrial relations, either directly such as NALGO, or more indirectly such as the Library Association, also have an important contribution to make to the workplace. Their ideas and perspectives help to illustrate current events and also their perceptions of their roles in the workplace. The four contained here have been chosen because of their range of involvement, and their differing perspectives on the whole area of industrial relations. They all reflect some of the issues outlined in Part One, and three of the organizations are directly concerned with the library and information profession. The purpose of this perspective is to provide just that – an overview of policies and practices from unions and related organizations.

The Library Association, although not a trade union (an ongoing debate!), does however play a very active part in the conditions of work relating to its members. It publishes information, provides advice, acts as a clearing house for information and is a very important part of the policy-making process. The overview here gives some clear examples of the involvement of the Association in grass roots issues.

Both NALGO and NATFHE represent large numbers of librarians and information workers among their membership, and so the case studies provide the background to their activities and examples of particular cases. The GMB has been included as an example of a union which has strong opinions and ideas on the future of unions and union membership. Even though it is not directly involved with librarians and information workers, many of those working in information and library services are members of the GMB, particularly manual workers in the public sector. The changes in practices within this union are important to managers working in the public sector, and also reflect many of the shifts in the political climate outlined in the Introduction.

9 The role of the Library Association *David Ruse*

As a professional body, the role of The Library Association in employee relations and relationships of people at work may not be immediately obvious. However, under the terms of its Royal Charter the Association is charged with a number of activities which have a direct bearing on this subject. The Royal Charter empowers the Association amongst other things to:

- promote the better management of library and information services
- promote the improvement of the knowledge, skills, position and the qualifications of librarians and information personnel
- provide appropriate services to members in furtherance of these objectives.

In the *Futures report* of 1985,[1] functions to support these Royal Charter objectives were identified as: providing advice on matters relating to employment and career development, and promoting guidelines of practice and guidelines for provision of services. Services identified included:

- activities to promote the skills of members amongst potential employers and clients
- the publication and promotion of recommendations on the status, conditions of service and salaries of librarians and information personnel regardless of their working environment
- publication of a medium for the advertising of vacancies in librarianship and information work
- the maintenance and promotion of a Code of Professional Conduct.

Whilst these functions and services were first described in the *Futures report*, they had been provided in one form or another for a long period of time. Indeed if one refers back to the *Library Association record* of the earlier parts of the century, one will find many examples of the Association's concern for the salaries and status of librarians. It is by no means a new phenomenon.

The Library Association believes in the skills, qualifications and expertise of library staff and regards these as essential to the quality of a library service. It is therefore not surprising that matters to do with the management and development of the staff of library and information services are a prime concern of the Association. As a professional body it has long had responsibilities and interests in the education, training and development of the workforce, including the award of qualifications and the maintenance of a register of Chartered Members, who are judged to be competent professionals. The Association advises employers and trade unions, members and others on all aspects of library staffing. Drawing upon examples of good practice it provides information and advice and devises guidelines.

The current activities of the Association in the sphere of employee relations are considerable. Perhaps the most obvious is the monitoring of advertised vacancies which are published in the fortnightly 'Vacancies supplement' to the *Library Association record* and elsewhere, to ensure that they conform to Association policy. The Association lays down criteria by which the salary, related conditions and structural position of posts are evaluated. If posts fail to meet the criteria then action is taken. This action normally takes the form of representations to the employer concerned in the hope that they will make changes to meet the Association's requirements. A recent example involved a national organization which advertised in the *Guardian* newspaper for a Librarian. The Association was concerned that an appropriate qualification was not an essential requirement for the job and that the salary quoted was considerably below the Association's recommendations. Indeed it was below comparable posts in the same organization, advertised in the same newspaper. Letters were sent to the organization encouraging it to review the position. The organization subsequently re-advertised the post, still on the same salary, and the Association made further representations. Only time will tell whether the organization has taken note of the Association's view. In extreme cases the Association will advise its members not to participate in the recruitment process for a particular post. This is known as boycotting. Full details of the Association's monitoring and boycotting procedure were given in an article in the *Record* in June 1988.[2] Whilst the Association's representations are rarely successful in respect of the particular post, there is evidence to suggest that in the longer term these representations do have a positive effect and improvements are made to meet the Association's criteria.

Another major area where the Association is involved in employee relations is in making recommendations on salaries and conditions of service for the various sectors of the library and information profession. These are produced annually in a series of printed salary guides which are widely distributed. Each guide contains recommendations concerning salaries, duties and responsibilities and other matters relating to the salary structure for the sector in question. The recommendations in the guide are based on current good practice.

The guide for public libraries contains a brief introduction which describes the national machinery for determining salary scales. It then identifies the specialist and general skills of librarians and the duties and responsibilities of library assistants. A framework of five levels of library staff is provided, with definitions of responsibility at each level. Recommended salary grades are attached to each of these levels, and an insert provides the current salary figures. Similar guides are available for the National Health Service, the Civil Service, academic and commercial libraries.

On a more general level, the Association considers and issues statements on a wide range of personnel-related topics. The Association's intention is to promote good employment practices in areas where there are particular problems relating to library and information services. Some recent examples of this include statements on the use of volunteers in welfare libraries[3] and on support for staff development and training.[4] Many library staff find it increasingly difficult to secure paid time off for training and development activities, partly because of the demise of staff training budgets and partly because of the particular problems faced by library staff in maintaining services to users if they are not at their place of work. The policy statement encourages employers to support positively the training and development of their staff. The benefits to employers of a well-motivated workforce which is up to date with current developments are described. Practical suggestions are made for employers to provide help, including making time available, the payment of fees and expenses and the creation of a supportive environment for staff.

Another example where particular problems have faced library staff is over the question of aggressive and unacceptable behaviour in libraries. Here the Association has produced valuable guidance notes and advice on preventing such behaviour in a publication entitled *Violence in libraries*.[5] The Association's advice treats the subject as a management issue and suggests a structured and supportive approach to dealing with the problem. Often, the fear of incidents is greater than the actual existence of them and so all library managers have a responsibility to address the issue. Many practical suggestions are made in the leaflet which also includes a model incident-reporting form. Despite some recent research findings which indicated that librarians had a very low stress factor, the incidence of violence reported to the Association demonstrates that the stress faced by library staff is increasing.

The Association is taking an increasing interest in equal opportunities. The overwhelming predominance of women in the profession (about 70%) is not reflected in the numbers of women who have achieved senior management positions. A similar situation arises in respect of people from various ethnic minorities and people with disabilities. The Library Association has monitored its own membership for equal opportunities purposes and this has revealed some valuable, but disturbing information. From an 81% return, 98% of members were of European origin and 75% were female. Members whose ethnic origins were African, Afro-Caribbean, Asian or Oriental made up the remaining 2% – very small numbers indeed. About 1% of members were disabled people. A full analysis of the monitoring was published in the *Record* in January 1989. Clearly the Association needs to do more to find out why so few people from ethnic minorities or with disabilities are recruited into the profession and why so few women achieve senior management positions. To help it do this, in 1987 the Association adopted an equal opportunities policy[6] and is in the process of carrying out various recommendations arising from this policy. In addition, an *Equal opportunities information pack* was issued in 1989[7] containing, amongst other things, documents on job sharing, recruitment, language and people with disabilities. New guidance notes are regularly added to the pack.

One major area of the Association's work, which is somewhat unusual in terms of the activities of professional associations, is the large amount of individual help and assistance which the Association gives to members who are facing difficulties or problems with some employment-related matter. The Association is regularly consulted by members for information, support and advice in respect of salaries, conditions of service and organizational problems. This advice is given freely on a confidential basis and can often be influential in securing change or improvement for the member and the service concerned. Some examples of this work are described below. In the National Health Service, a large number of members are underpaid for the level of work which they are performing. The Association regularly receives requests for advice and support from members who are trying to improve their position. In such cases, the Association will provide advice on tactics, points to emphasize and things to avoid when submitting claims for regrading. Whilst every case is treated on its merits, there are many common points and so the Association has produced a leaflet[8] containing the basic information. As well as advising members, the Association will provide letters of support for members. These will set out the Association's view about the salary and duties of a post and can be used as supporting documentation when a claim is submitted.

In other cases, members will ask for advice on things like pensions, redundancy terms and other conditions of service issues.

In each case, the Association will provide support and advice, referring as necessary to other agencies.

In the college sector, help is frequently given to underpaid members in the ways indicated earlier. However, a frequent occurrence is for posts to be regraded when someone leaves. In these cases, the regrading is often downwards. The Association will make representations, presenting reasoned arguments about the level of work involved and drawing on comparative data as appropriate.

Many changes are management-led. Over two-thirds of public-library authorities have had structural or organizational changes over the last three years. Library managers frequently approach the Association for comparative data, state-of-the-art assessments and other information which they can use to support or inform their own initiatives. For example, recent enquiries about the salary grades of local studies librarians across the country were answered from the Association's files.

To underpin the Association's casework, a number of statistical surveys are regularly carried out. These surveys seek to establish the number, grades and duties and qualifications of library staff working in different parts of the profession. The public library census and the college library surveys are regularly carried out and there are plans for a survey of school libraries. Some sectors of the profession are surveyed by other groups and the results are used by the Association to help members in these fields. In many cases this survey work is unique and therefore of great value to employers, trade unions and individual members.

In all of its activities in this field, the Association maintains close links with the trade-union movement. It has a formal relationship with the Association of University Teachers, with the Institution of Professionals, Managers and Specialists (IPMS) and with the National and Local Government Officers Association (NALGO). Observers from the Association's staff regularly attend meetings of the NATFHE Libraries Section and the FUMPO Libraries Section. Many members of the Association are also active in their trade union at local or regional or national level. Indeed in 1988 the President of NALGO was a librarian. The formal relationships with the trade unions at national level are very useful in exchanging information and ideas for the mutual benefit of members of both organizations. Early in 1988, NALGO's local government section decided to undertake a major new initiative for its members working in public libraries. This began with a weekend workshop in Manchester for library stewards. The Library Association made a major contribution to this event, staff from headquarters giving papers and leading discussion groups. The outcome of the weekend provided an agenda for NALGO action in the future. One element of this is a new publication, Library staff: guidelines for action[9] produced in conjunction with the Library Association. The guidelines are intended to assist branches in negotiating improvements to the grading and conditions of service of library staff and to aid branch organization and recruitment. There is therefore a very positive and constructive relationship with this major public-sector trade union.

Recent changes to the status of polytechnics and some higher-education colleges have also provided a role for The Library Association. Members working in the libraries of these institutions may be on lecturers' salaries and conditions of service or on local government salaries and conditions. In some cases they are on a combination of these. This has caused problems and resentment in the past. However, it is likely that there will be a major rationalization of pay and conditions in these institutions over the next couple of years. Library staff form only a very small element of the total staff affected and NALGO and NATFHE, the two trade unions involved, would probably not have had library staff high on their list of priorities. However, the Library Association has engaged both unions in tripartite discussions at national level, which has served to highlight the issues affecting library staff and allowed discussion of possible solutions with the key officials who will be negotiating pay and conditions for the future. This would not have happened without The Library Association which can provide expertise, information and an organization to support such initiatives. The outcome is still to be decided, but at least the Association is setting the agenda for change rather than trying to fit library staff to a set of conditions devised for other groups.

It has often been suggested that The Library Association itself should form a trade union for library staffs. Whilst there would be several advantages to such a development, particularly the fact that the union would be dedicated to the needs and interest of library staffs, there would also be the major disadvantage that such a union would first of all have to recruit members from existing trade unions, which would be met with great hostility; secondly it would have to establish negotiating rights on behalf of its members with various employers' organizations, a highly unlikely development particularly at the present time; and thirdly, it would have to establish a local and regional network of union officials who could support individual members in a far more detailed way than the Association's present resources allow. One inevitable consequence of this would be a major increase in subscriptions. Another major disadvantage would be the loss of the ability for the Association to speak with equal effect to employers' organizations as well as trade unions. At the moment the Association can speak objectively as a professional association concerned with standards of provision and practice. It is therefore listened to by employers both locally and nationally. The Association can also speak to the relevant trade unions on the same basis. I believe this to be more effective than for the Association to become a trade union.

The Association's links with the employers are less strong than those with the employees' organizations. However, it does have very strong links with library managers' organizations such as the various chief librarians' groups and with individual chief librarians whom it can influence by way of statements, advice or information. The chief librarians themselves can be influential in their own organizations. There is need for the Association to establish more adequate relationships with employers' organizations like the Local Government Management Board, the Committee of Vice-Chancellors and Principals and the Committee of Directors of Polytechnics and I hope that the Association will make progress in this area before too long.

Because the Association is at the centre of a major professional information network, it is able to monitor changes taking place within the profession in a unique way. This enables the Association to collect and provide information and advice on all matters to do with employee relations affecting library and information staff. Information on salaries, grading, staffing structures and other matters all come to the attention of the Association in one way or another. In a time of rapid organizational and environmental change, the Association should therefore form an integral part of an individual's network for information and advice.

The Library Association is essentially a membership organization. It is 25,000 people. Obviously for the Association to be effective it has a structure and a paid staff. It is useful to record how employee-relations issues are handled within that structure. The Association is governed by an elected Council which has a number of standing subject committees. One of these is the Employment Committee and it deals with all matters relating to the staffing of library and information services. This committee has a number of Panels which advise it on activities in particular parts of the profession. They are the Academic Libraries Panel, the Public and School Libraries Panel, and the Special Libraries Panel. There is also an Equal Opportunities Panel. This committee and these panels are supported in their work by a team of staff within the Professional Practice Division of the secretariat. As well as servicing the committees, the staff provide, collect and analyse the vast range of information and advice referred to earlier. In order to promote the Association's work in the employee-relations field, a leaflet was recently produced entitled *How we can help you*. This, along with *Trade union news*, a periodic newsletter aimed at library trades unionists, and regular news and articles in the *Library Association record* are some of the ways in which the Association informs its membership of developments and of the services available. In addition, a number of the specialist groups of the Association take an interest in employee-relations issues. Particular reference should be made to the Personnel, Training and Education Group which has only recently embraced 'Personnel' within its title and will clearly be developing its interest in this wider area over the next few years.

As a professional body concerned with standards of library and information practice and provision, the Library Association recognizes that staffing is fundamental to effectiveness. It has always taken and will continue to take a keen interest in any activities which have an effect on staff. Its activities in the employee relations field can be summed up as promoting good employment practices by providing information and advice to managers, employees, trade unions, employers and individual members on any matters relating to the staffing of libraries.

References

1 Library Association, *Final report on the Futures Working Party*, London, LA, 1985.
2 Ruse, David, 'Good jobs and bad jobs', *Library Association record*, **90** (6), 1988, 343–4.
3 Library Association, *The use of volunteers in welfare libraries*, London, LA, 1987.
4 Library Association, *Support for staff development and training*, London, LA, 1987.
5 Library Association, *Violence in libraries: preventing aggressive and unacceptable behaviour in libraries*, London, LA, 1987.
6 Library Association, *Equal opportunities policy statement*, London, LA, 1987.
7 Library Association, *Equal opportunities information pack*, London, LA, 1989.
8 Library Association, *Submitting a regrading claim in the NHS*, London, LA, 1988.
9 NALGO, *Library staff: guidelines for action*, London, NALGO, 1989.

10 Industrial relations: a NALGO perspective John Findlay

Political and economic pressure on the trade-union movement during the 1980s and early 1990s has obliged them to develop more sophisticated responses to industrial relations problems. Trade unions must of course sustain their primary responsibilities of tackling injustices in employment and promoting their members' pay and conditions; but there is now a much more widespread grasp of the underlying political forces which can generate industrial relations difficulties. Cutbacks in expenditure, for example, imposed upon local authorities by central government, have been a central force in developing a more considered trade union response in the public sector. Trade union sanctions against an individual local authority implementing such cutbacks might sometimes be successful in resisting reductions in services or jobs, but it may well do nothing to undermine the government policy that is imposing those cutbacks; and it may indeed on occasion strengthen the government's public relations hand.

Trade unions have learnt in these circumstances to couple their 'firefighting' response at local and national level with wider political initiatives aimed at winning public support and either securing changes in government policy or resisting its implementation. Some trade unions, particularly those with political affiliations, have of course undertaken this sort of approach for some time; but there can be no doubt that in seeking to resolve industrial-relations problems, trade unions have sometimes disregarded wider political considerations and often neglected public opinion. Now there is a real determination to tackle political forces which impinge unfavourably upon the employment and working conditions of members. There can be no doubt about the difficulty of this task, nor about the scale of resources or quality of organization and leadership which will be required of trade unions if they are to succeed. Equally, however, it is absolutely clear that in the present circumstances the resolution of industrial relations problems can be achieved only in the context of political pressures and that responses relating solely to the individual employer will be inadequate.

The library service is a classic example of this. The service is afflicted by a range of industrial relations problems, some generated by local mismanagement, others by political neglect. In this chapter I shall examine each of these industrial relations problems and suggest that their resolution will not be achieved unless we recognize their relationship with wider considerations such as the political status of the library service.

Pay

Library work has always been badly paid. Most library assistants and other unqualified staff are paid on NJC Scale 1 providing a salary range (in 1990) of £4,707 to £8,367. They are low paid in absolute terms. Their salaries fall below the 'decency threshold' set by the Council of Europe. (£9,330, 1.1.91). Qualified librarians typically commence on Scale 4 (£9,795 – £10,950) but starting-points are frequently as low as Scale 3 (£8,943 – £9,600) or Scale 2 (£8,367 – £8,775).

A Deputy Branch Librarian may proceed to a salary on Scale 4 or Scale 5 and a Branch Librarian may proceed to the dizzy heights of Scale 6 or even SO1. As we shall see later, higher salaries can be achieved in a few senior managerial and specialist posts, but these are a very small proportion of the total workforce. To those familiar with local government, the mismatch between grading in the library service and that in some other departments is immediately obvious: there is a general discrepancy of about one or two grades between the practice in the library structure and that in mainstream local government. Recruits to other local government services can often expect high salary points on entry and a better main grade for the standard qualified job. It could be argued that library assistants are no more badly paid than basic-grade staff elsewhere within the service; but the work typically undertaken by a library assistant in practice contains major aspects of contact with the public and of self-direction within an overall policy framework, which in other posts would be reflected in an improved grading.

Working conditions

One area of particular grievance among library workers is the requirement to work unsocial hours. Although some compensation is given in terms of time off in lieu or overtime, the general attitude of local authorities seems to be that the primary obligation of library workers is to meet the exigencies of a service which has traditionally (although no longer) been based on six-day opening. The trade union view is that the working week in local government is Monday to Friday, broadly from 9 to 5, and that additional working must be with the consent of the individual and, if worked, remunerated at premium rates. Restrictions on funding for the library service have, of course, led to reduced opening and it could be argued that unsocial hours have become less of a problem as a result. However, the real saving achieved by reduced opening hours is that fewer staff are required. In general there has been a reduction in overall staffing levels corresponding to reduced opening hours. In many cases staffing levels have been cut even further and many library workers now express particular concern about the impact on the service provided to the public and the increased personal stress and risk of violence for staff forced by reduced staffing levels to work on their own. Serious assaults in libraries are not commonplace, but the nuisance and personal risk often faced daily by library workers, especially in inner-city areas and in the evenings, are very considerable.

Training and qualification

NALGO is wholly committed to training and qualification for local government staff and committed to ensuring equal access to training and development of career opportunities, to enable all employees to develop their work and their career. Training and qualification should be a supporting part of that process. Training and qualification within the library service seem, however, to have a distinct flavour of exclusiveness about them. There is an absolute distinction between 'qualified' and 'unqualified' staff. It is commonplace within the service to talk of 'professional' and 'non-professional' staff, even (in less guarded moments) of 'unprofessional' staff! Library assistants are collectively described as 'support', 'auxiliary' or 'ancillary'. These harsh distinctions have no place in a flexible and responsible public organization which encourages a pattern of career development to the advantage of both the service and the individual. The problem has, of course, been recognized by many within the service and some considerable steps have been taken in developing alternative routes of qualification. Nevertheless, the requirement for qualifications within the library service continues to be something that *prevents* people from undertaking certain duties, rather than providing them with the skills with which to undertake their job more effectively. Some progress has undoubtedly been made; it is not so long since one major municipal library had separate entrances for senior and junior staff!

Career structures

Closely related to this issue of training and qualification is the inadequacy of career opportunity for many library workers. Although we have seen the development of some overlap in grading terms between qualified and unqualified staff in recent years, it remains the case that library assistants continue to be perceived and graded according to the title and status of their post, regardless of the real responsibility they may be undertaking. There is, moreover, a tendency within the library service to assume that progression in terms of training and qualification can only be in library skills.

In the library service, as in any other branch of local government, there is a wide range of managerial, supervisory and other organizational skills which can and should be developed and properly recognized. In other local government services, there is a wide variety of administrative, financial, personnel and similar functions which are open to suitably qualified people who may or may not be qualified in the primary professional function of that particular department. There is indeed considerable career progression in these fields across different departments. In library work this seems not to be so. It seems impossible for library assistants to make progress towards more senior levels of administrative, financial or personnel functions which generally are not available to staff as promotions unless they are qualified librarians.

Even if this problem were to be overcome there would still be another major problem of career development. Like a number of other areas where the service is provided directly to the public, the library service suffers from its 'flat pyramid' organizational structure. Large numbers of staff are required at library-service-point level, in contact with the public, to ensure proper delivery of the service. The management hierarchy above that level is disproportionately small compared to some other services within local government. This clearly restricts the opportunities for career development for individual workers and it is commonplace for library staff to spend the bulk of their career in the same level of work, with no real opportunity to move into better graded and more responsible positions which they would be perfectly able to undertake.

Equal opportunities
The industrial relations issues identified so far are, of course, significantly typical of those areas of employment where the majority of the workforce are women. Trade unions have no doubt about the impact on pay and conditions in work which is undertaken predominantly by women. The pattern is quite clear: the pay of women in non-manual jobs in the United Kingdom continues to be only some 70% of that of men. In areas of employment where women form the majority of the workforce, such as nursing or library work, then the general level of pay is substantially less than in the mainstream. There can be no excuse for this. Local authorities cannot claim to be eradicating inequality of opportunity if they sustain grading levels and structures which are themselves based on outdated attitudes towards women and women's pay. Poor grading in the library service is at best a failure by local authorities to recognize that their assumptions about the 'rate for the job' in library work are outdated and unfairly discriminatory, or at worst

that some local authorities still make unlawful assumptions about pay for work done mainly by women.

A related issue under this heading is equality of opportunity in promotion. It is improper in a service in which women predominate that the overwhelming majority of chief librarians are men and that there are fewer women than men in senior managerial positions generally. One senior librarian once explained this phenomenon to me by pointing out that male librarians were under greater financial obligations and therefore made the extra effort that was required to secure these senior and better-paid posts, a point of view which does seem to reinforce my comments about outdated attitudes. There is no doubt, however, that among women library workers there is very considerable conviction that men find it easier to achieve promotion, that inadequate training opportunities exist and, perhaps most seriously of all, there continues to be built-in discrimination in which senior male managers in the library service continue to appoint male subordinates. In some cases this is no doubt due to outright sexism, but in NALGO's experience it is more often a less conscious form of discrimination. Local authorities clearly need to do more in conjunction with trade unions to develop equal opportunities programmes which will seek to develop managers' self-awareness and encourage the promotion of women to senior posts.

Pay and conditions: the NALGO response
For many years there was a nationally prescribed grading for libraries in the conditions of service determined by the National Joint Council. National negotiations continue to be fundamental to the achievement of good industrial relations, but it became increasingly apparent that national grading prescriptions for particular groups of staff such as librarians were no longer productive. The purpose of national grading prescriptions is to ensure that all local authorities conform to a national standard. Once that standard has been achieved the national prescription can constrain, rather than facilitate, grading development. Any attempt to improve national grading prescriptions meets with major resistance from those authorities which pay only at that level and with disinterest from those authorities which have already disregarded it and pay at improved levels.

The prescription thus becomes a statement of the lowest applicable grading level and is often used by local authorities to resist pressure from trade unions locally when they seek to improve the grading structure. As a result of this NALGO has moved away from national grading prescriptions in many areas in order to remove the constraint and allow gradings to float to their natural level locally. This has led to some movement in many areas, but generally speaking grading levels remain low. A major initiative is now under way to promote local grading improvements. In liaison with The Library Association a series of local and regional initiatives is being established to ensure close consultation through joint workshops and the production of joint briefing packs. National material is being produced to assist branches in negotiating major improvements in grading and conditions of service. We anticipate that these claims will not be restricted simply to issues of pay and conditions of service, but will also have an impact on the way in which the local library service is run, including questions of training, qualification, career opportunity and equal opportunities.

The wider task
There is major work to be done at all levels in combating poor grading and employment practice among local library authorities. We have a clear duty to provide national coordination for local claims aimed at improving grades and conditions of service training and opportunity. It seems clear to us, however, that trade union efforts at local level will be hampered from the start by the neglect of local authorities and the threat from central government. Some local authorities pride themselves on their library service and, though industrial relations difficulties will inevitably occur from time to time, at least there is a real commitment to libraries which is in some cases reflected in the pay and conditions of service which their staff enjoy. In many other local authorities the state of the libraries and the pay and conditions of library workers reflect the authority's lack of real commitment to the library service. In either case, local councillors will not regard librarians as high on their list of political priorities when they are extolling the virtues of their authority or, more particularly, when they are looking round for areas in which to make savings. In setting out their virtues to the electorate, local authorities will draw attention to their schools, colleges, to their sports facilities, to their economic regeneration schemes, to their road building, but not in general to their libraries. There does indeed seem to be a complacency among both the electorate and most local-authority leaders about the importance and function of libraries. Libraries are generally unquestioned features of local council provision. Whether they are widely used or not, both local authorities and the community seem to expect them to be there. This attitude has allowed local library services to run with some considerable autonomy and to achieve in some areas very great progress in terms of public service, but it has also in general led to poor standards

of pay and grading.

Public complacency about libraries does seem to suggest quite strongly that there is very considerable support for libraries among the general public and this is a feature which could no doubt be exploited a great deal more than it is. But complacency about a public service carries great dangers. Local political leaders are understandably more sensitive to those areas of service provision which are of immediate concern to the community, such as schools, transport, social services, roads. Complacency about the library service means that it is at risk. Until recently reductions in service have not led to a public perception of the library service being in jeopardy. Cutbacks have been regarded as unavoidable measures. Local authorities, recognizing that reductions of this sort in the library service had not created a major public outcry, have moved steadily down the road of cutbacks, closures, charging and reduced facilities. Only when major closures occur has there been a wider public outcry. This trend in local authority thinking has now reached the point where among local authority politicians there is an increasing view that libraries may not be such a vital service after all, and that the assumption that they should always exist might be mistaken. One might expect such attitudes to be restricted to local authority leaders of a particular political complexion, but this is not so. There is a worrying trend among a number of otherwise sympathetic local councillors that the library service is under-used, and that, if it is used, it is mainly by the retired middle class, who in any case do not form a major part of their constituency. The logic in this position is that the library service should be thoroughly reviewed, stripped of features which do not provide value for money for the whole community, reorganized to ensure higher-level service among deprived communities (e.g. through a shift to mobile libraries) and finally lose major resources to more politically rewarding areas such as education and housing. That these attitudes may be unjust, ill-informed and outrageous, NALGO would agree. But there can be no denying that there is strong pressure in local government, whether brought in by financial constraint or right wing dogma, for libraries to be examined very closely and any shortcomings no doubt exploited for reasons of political expediency.

This potential destabilization of the library service was hugely reinforced by the Green Paper[1] and the powers in the Local Government and Housing Act 1989,[2] despite the Minister's embarrassment at climbing down, in early 1989, from his commitment to a premium book service. The impact of the Major succession has yet to emerge, but there is no doubt that the Thatcher administration was strongly committed to applying its political dogma of the market, privatization and centralization to all the public services. It was the turn of libraries. It was easy to be cynical about the task of the Minister for the Arts in having to show, as a loyal Minister, that he too could subject his portfolio to the privatizing dogma. It was no reason, however, for underestimating the enormous danger which faces the library service today. Many believe that the former Prime Minister, responsible for setting the tone and pace of so much of the government's action, could have some attachment to libraries, born out of her own personal experience. No one could doubt the pressures from the purist libertarian wing of the ruling government party, whose attitude continues to be that if you need a book or other information resource, you should buy it; and if you can't afford to buy it, then that it is an incentive to earn more money.

NALGO's view is that government powers established in the legislation arising from the Green Paper, coupled with the re-think in many local authorities about the relative political value of libraries, will pose a major threat to the library service as we know it today. It could certainly lead to major reductions in the service and to widespread closures.

NALGO believes that the library service's future growth and development and the fulfilment of its obligation to provide a service to the whole community will depend on driving home a very clear political message: that there is widespread support for libraries among the public, not least among many people who support the present government, and that cutbacks and privatization of the library service would lead to an unacceptable removal of a major component of the social fabric of this country. By developing that message NALGO believes that the library service can become more actively supported and less vulnerable to cutbacks and political fashion. A higher profile for the library service in political terms is obviously a high-risk option. The approach will not succeed if the service cannot stand up to the full glare of political examination. Nevertheless, the development of a more acute political presence for the library service is vital if it is to escape neglect and consequent vulnerability. Re-establishing libraries as a popular and fundamental cornerstone of local public provision can in the longer term provide the only route to better funding, improved services and, not least, an end to at least some of the industrial relations problems which beset the service.

References
1 *Financing our public library service: four subjects for debate*, London, HMSO, 1988 (Green Paper: Cm 324).

2 *Local Government and Housing Act,* London, HMSO, 1989.

Further reading
Byrne, T., *Local government in Britain,* 3rd ed., London, Penguin, 1985.

11 The NATFHE perspective *David Triesman*

Introduction
Making predictions about developments in industrial relations is notoriously difficult. Change has been so rapid that most observers and practitioners acknowledge that few would have foreseen the full pattern of events over the last 15 years.

Most accounts of recent change start from the election of a Conservative Government in 1979. It is tempting to do so. After all, the Conservatives have carried through five major changes in trade union legislation which have circumscribed dramatically the activities of unions in the conduct of negotiations and disputes and the ordering of their internal government. The culmination of the Conservative drive to change the balance of power decisively in favour of employers is, perhaps, that, having established legally enforceable balloting requiring majority votes before dispute action, they have now made it illegal to exert discipline over those who ignore a positive decision to take action made by the workforce involved.

The net impact of the legislation is that the law on industrial relations has become increasingly impenetrable to practitioners. Indeed, it is now so opaque that both managers and unions await precedents in the courts in order to find out what the law means, a process frustrating to practitioners if highly lucrative to lawyers.

The legislation and associated legal instruments have been accompanied by the abolition of bargaining rights of any kind for English and Welsh schoolteachers and the banning of unions altogether at the Government Communications Headquarters. Each major effort at privatization, especially if accompanied by competitive tendering, has threatened if not disrupted long-standing bargaining arrangements and trade-union organization. Finally, where the Government is the employer or in those areas of employment where central funding is the basis for pay (local authorities and nationalized industries, for example), the Government has tried to show the private sector by example what can be done to depress salary levels, eliminate national pay rates and increase 'flexibility' in working practices. Ironically, whilst 'private-sector methods' are pleaded in aid of such developments, it is evident from many ministerial speeches to the CBI and City of London luminaries and, particularly, on the occasions when the Budget or Autumn Expenditure White Paper is presented, it is the public sector that is shown to demonstrate exemplary reductions in 'inflationary labour costs' to the private-sector employers.

The catalogue of reverses for trade unions may appear to justify the view that things began to change in 1979. The view is too simple. For the great strengths of trade unions – what Robert Taylor[1] called *the fifth estate* – to have been downgraded in national political life so rapidly suggests deeper changes in economic and social structure. That the reverses for unions have been so popular among trade union members who express their alienation from the decision-making processes of their own unions, must prompt a deeper analysis. Even if stimulated by the mass media, the Conservative Government used a disgruntlement already there. They did not create it.

This paper considers some of these underlying trends and describes how they have affected changes in employment in post-school education, including the employment of librarians.

Forces below the surface
A brief account of significant change is always prone to crudeness, although four trends can be recognized.

First, there has been extensive dismemberment of the key production and extraction industries which were highly unionized. Not only did this increase unemployment, sapping the numerical strength and confidence of unions, but it shifted the power balance in the TUC. The great traditional battalions of organized workers are no longer the exclusive focus of power, having partially given way to service-industry, white-collar and high-technology unions. However, in those latter industries employers tend to be smaller and the extent of unionization far lower. Thus the strength of unionism has declined as a result of changes in industrial structure.

Second, in part taking advantage of a weakening of union power, the Government have successfully reduced the strong popular sentiment invested in collective provision of services, in the area which Mr Jack Jones as General Secretary of the Transport and General Workers' Union called 'the social wage'. The link between the welfare of education, the health service, public housing, the social services, the arts and so on, and the unions should not be underestimated. It is not just that unions were so important in the post-war settlement that created the modern form of these social services. There is a powerful ideological link between collective social provision and collective forms of political and economic organization. The values of collectivism with its historical emphasis on group support for individuals contrasts strongly with the values of a free market in which individual 'customers' shape the aggregate character of the market-place precisely because they act as individuals rather than collectively. When the Government is seen to go too far in dismantling collective provision, as it is seen to be in the NHS, there is adverse public response. That cannot disguise the fact, however, that the extent and pace of the movement to private provision have been considerable whatever the outcry. At base, Government ability to attack vulnerable social provision relies on the reality that it has become vulnerable over a long period.

Third, these social changes have engendered individualism to a point where it is legitimate to celebrate selfishness, popular to put oneself first. Even the geographical areas that have prospered reflect that change. You could do better for yourself if you migrated in the direction of prosperity in the selfish South-East. More social responses like regional aid directed to even out the geographical imbalances has all but ceased. Individuals should not, it appears, be foolish enough to live north of Milton Keynes or west of Exeter.

Last, the regulation of working relations has gone through marked oscillations. Between 1974 and 1979, two major pieces of legislation considerably increased the authority of unions and individual workers, especially where those workers were represented collectively. A variety of methods for resolving disputes by conciliation and arbitration emerged and came to be regarded as viable alternatives to disputes. Whether the disputes which nonetheless emerged in the winter of 1978-9 ended this approach or the view grew among employers that the rights of unions had been too greatly extended in 1978, the introduction of the fiver major Tory Acts represents not just change, but a wild swing in the balance. This process of violent swings has made the nuts-and-bolts regulation of industrial relations unreliable – unreliable to everyone involved.

These trends may seem large-scale and national but this is only part of their character. They alter the most local and individual relations at work. In the last seven years it has sometimes appeared that unions have not looked outward at these changes in order to arrive at a strategy for dealing with them or for halting them. Perhaps all beleaguered organizations run the risk of becoming introverted, but if that is true, they are in the additional danger of seeming increasingly ineffective or irrelevant to their own members.

Employment in post-school education

The trends described have had impact in education, as in other sectors of the economy, and education unions (not just teacher unions but all those with members employed in education) have experienced the back-wash.

Whilst this section of this chapter considers a part of education in which many librarians are employed, it is important to note first the changes through which schools are going. Briefly, schoolteachers have suffered a depression of earnings compared with occupational groups with similar patterns of qualification, training and experience. They have lost the right, other than in Scotland, to negotiate terms and conditions of employment. In the Education Reform Act 1988, the Secretary of State for Education and Science has accumulated rights to determine in some detail what is taught in a national core curriculum, an 'innovation' impeded only by a severe shortage of teachers qualified to teach much of it. Thus, not only has the Government taken control of what is to be done, but has control of how it is to be done, and under what working arrangements. The final twist has been to provide a basis upon which local education authorities lose their remaining powers so that school governors can become the employers.

This last change is profound for industrial relations because it means that governors at the most local level will gradually assume powers to set all the main terms of employment for all staff, not only teachers. There could be no more basic challenge to national bargaining and it will affect every school employee. In the case of manual workers in schools, many have lost jobs, as services like school meals and cleaning have gone to private contractors – usually non-unionized and paying below the nationally negotiated rates.

The media, in focusing on schools, have yet to see the extent of the transition in post-school education produced by the 1988 Act. Changes to universities other than in their funding council (the Universities Funding Council) are not so great as those to polytechnics and colleges of further education. As important employers of library staff, it is worth considering the changes in some detail.

Until June 1988, it was possible to describe the long-term employment characteristics in local-authority colleges with a degree of precision and certainty. The institutions had been governed by the Further Education Regulations (1975–7) which regulated the reorganization of colleges of education, provisions for premises and courses, the award of grants, payment of fees, expenditure on equipment and the provision of sufficient qualified teaching staff to provide adequate instruction in the courses provided. Whilst these Regulations were replaced by new Education (Schools and Further Education) Regulations from 1981, introduced in order to avoid impeding the introduction of tertiary education systems, many of the rubrics have continued to provide a sound organizational basis. Inevitably this had implications for the organization of work.

The pay and conditions of staff have similarly been based on arrangements with considerable maturity and, it may be said, a reputation for reliability. Non-teaching staff have been for the most part subject to pay and conditions of service schemes negotiated by the appropriate National Joint Council for Local Authorities' Administrative, Professional, Technical and Clerical Services, or by the National Joint Council for Local Authorities' Services as appropriate. Lecturers have their pay and conditions negotiated in the National Joint Council for Further Education Lecturers in England and Wales, a body which assumed responsibility for the negotiations conducted in the Burnham FE Committee before 1987. All the national agreements appear in handbooks – the *Purple book* for APT&C staff, the *Buff book* for manual staff and the *Silver book* for lecturers. The constitutions, rates of pay, conditions of service, grading criteria and other NJC decisions, together with details of local arrangements for negotiation like the Provincial Councils (which do not affect lecturers and researchers), are to be found in these multi-coloured books. (They are listed in section 5).

All of these arrangements are emphasized because they have provided stability in employment. It was broadly true that employees in Cumbria or Cornwall were equally part of the same national scheme. With this came the advantage that for professional occupational groups recruitment and retention of staff occurred in the national market-place. Local employers could not undercut the pay rate nor impose detrimental working practices. This feature of the employment system was common among staff in general, although it is important to note that it was sometimes tested when it was not clear to which professional group a member of staff belonged. Perhaps the best example occurred with librarians who had a teaching commitment and were often designated 'tutor librarians'. Pragmatic decisions were required to determine whether such a member of staff was to be paid and have their conditions organized under the lecturers' NJC or the NJC for APT&C staff. Whilst employers favoured the latter as it reduced the cost to them of employing a tutor librarian, those in these posts frequently made the claim that a half or more of their work was lecturing and that this provided an entitlement to lecturing salaries and conditions. It is doubtful whether this dilemma has ever been satisfactorily resolved and many tutor librarians found themselves with lecturer's salaries and APT&C staff conditions. The posts in question are usually described as 'hybrid' and the two unions covering lecturers (NATFHE) and APT&C staff (NALGO) have a 'hybrid posts agreement' between them. If teaching comprises 50% or more of the job, the post is in NATFHE's sphere of influence and every effort is made to achieve lecturing pay and conditions. If teaching is less than half the job, it is in NALGO's sphere of influence and should attract APT&C pay and conditions.

It will be appreciated that pragmatic judgements of this kind are both created by and rely upon a stable set of national agreements to which all parties can turn.

The Education Reform Act 1988[2] changed all these systems. The test of their durability is about to start. In higher education in the polytechnics and colleges, all institutions above the very smallest and with 55% or more of advanced-level work have been removed from the local-authority sector. They have been placed under the auspices of the Polytechnics and Colleges Funding Council (PCFC) which, for funding and planning purposes, replaces the National Advisory Body (NAB). From an employment point of view, the largest change is that over 80 institutions formerly within LEAs become employers in their own right, taking full legal responsibility for the employment of their own staff. Although public money remains at the heart of PCFC funding, the status of the institutions is that they are corporations. In short, they now have a quasi-private status.

Two issues emerged immediately. First, because the LEAs are no longer employers, the national bargaining machinery in which the LEAs are the employers' side lost any authority for determining the pay and conditions of staff. Second, each employer needed to find new ways of settling future pay and conditions for its staff. These two facts are expressed in the new contracts received by all staff, including librarians, in the higher-education corporations (HECs), as they are called. One safeguard of enormous importance accompanies the transition from the LEA to the HEC. Under Section 127 of the 1988 Act, employees are entitled to have their existing contracts with all current terms and conditions transferred to the 'new' employer.

Of course, this safeguards only the immediate position and unions have had to consider the best way of dealing with over 80 new HECs. Bargaining with each would be time-consuming and create considerable anomalies, although there is evidence in other sectors of the economy that employers find this more disruptive than the unions. It was certainly the Government's preferred option, however, because there is a strong ideological commitment to breaking up national bargaining, largely in the belief that rates outside the South-East of England can be depressed below existing national rates. Such a proposition was never practicable, especially for approximately 50 of the institutions that are far too small for a free-standing bargaining operation or even a significant personnel department.

After many months of negotiation, in April 1989 a new national bargaining machinery was agreed for the new PCFC sector where national agreements made will be 'implemented in good faith' by the individual employers. Since the system of national bargaining which is superseded depended on the employers (the free-standing LEAs) being bound in honour to national agreement, the status of national agreements should not be significantly weakened. Given that this is not a good period in which to wear rose-coloured spectacles, from a union viewpoint it is necessary to add that an individual employing HEC which fails to 'implement in good faith' will find itself in the sights of some heavy artillery. Thus the new machinery has the capacity to avoid conflict but it remains to be seen whether prevailing macho styles of management will be dampened by employer agreement to take part in collective bargaining at national level. Some local agreements have already taken place.

The new national machinery, the Polytechnics and Colleges National Negotiating Committee, will undoubtedly experience a stronger push by the larger employers (the major polytechnics) for more local determination of conditions, and this is now happening. It appears likely that they will take an aggressive view of harmonizing working arrangements across groups of staff, in which case it would not be altogether surprising if teaching librarians found themselves in the firing-line with employers attempting to move them decisively toward administrative grades. Both the changes in bargaining machinery and the likely challenges to staff demonstrate the degree of doubt that replaces the more stable arrangements of the last decades. In particular, they illustrate the shift from national schemes now sought by the Government. Many new contracts at senior levels have recently been negotiated independently.

If these changes are dramatic, they will certainly be matched by those still to occur in further education. The colleges which have not been removed from LEAs into the PCFC sector will be removed just as decisively in fact if not in theory. Broadly these colleges undertake the non-advanced post-school work including adult education. They retain just over 10% of the advanced work. In the last eight years they have been increasingly oriented towards the kind of vocational preparation required by the then Training Agency. Educationalists, whether lecturers, librarians or other staff, have commented on the paucity of resources available for this work which discourages the use of libraries, librarians and other educational resources for the young people in the schemes.

Although the impact of the Training Agency (now the Training Enterprise and Education Directorate) has been significant in educational terms, it is beginning to be dwarfed by the 1990's organizational mutation. The 1988 Act provides that college governing bodies will assume responsibility for the hire and fire of staff, that they will control the budget of the college and that they can make all decisions on the grading of new staff (or staff when they are promoted). Much of the detail for these operations is set out in a DES Circular (9/88) which introduces some remarkable innovations. The key departure from common sense is that technically staff will remain the employees of an LEA but the decision to hire or fire them is not only an independent right of the governors but the LEA may not interfere in those decisions about 'LEA staff'. Consequently, if the governors dismiss someone unfairly, the LEA may not interfere but is responsible as the employer and will generally foot the compensation bill.

Of almost equivalent peculiarity is the provision that whilst pay scales and employment arrangements are to be set by national negotiation, the governors may place new staff where they see fit in the scale system and issue job descriptions for staff without impediment. It is not hard to see clashes both between governors' decisions and the national schemes for pay and conditions, and in arrangements adopted in colleges that may be near neighbours.

This could drive LEAs out of the major area of negotiating staff pay and conditions. Many union negotiators believe that whilst the LEAs will not welcome this consequence, they are victims of their own determination to please the Government by hugely increasing the scope for local rather than national determination of pay and conditions. Initially the LEAs sought a shift from national control to local LEA control but the shell they fired had such velocity that it has greatly overshot its target and it will be college governors who gain control. The role of the LEA could hardly be smaller. When this tactical blunder is added to the loss of bargaining, and the opting-out option in the schools, many LEAs will have the smallest level of responsibility at any time in their history. It is questionable whether they can survive this walk in the desert.

Almost inevitably, the unions will attempt several tactics which may prevent wholesale damage. First, they are certain to fight to retain as great a national framework as possible, rather than allow disintegration of agreements forged over many years. Among the options to be considered must be whether the governing bodies should themselves be represented on the employers' side in national bargaining. Whilst there is no mechanism to accomplish this at the time of writing, it appears unlikely that governors will or will need to feel committed to national deals in which they have no hand. Second, all unions are bound to increase their local effort. Local negotiators will have to be trained and provided with the back-up that negotiators need when dealing with employers.

The latter approach may pose different problems for different unions, so it is to be expected that they will adopt different solutions. For example, in an average college there will be about 200 full-time lecturers and a large number of part-time lecturers and about 85% will be NATFHE members. Traditionally that has formed the basis of NATFHE's organization – the workplace Branch. Although the character of Branch life would change, it is relatively easy to see this as a basis for industrial relations activity. Other unions are organized on an LEA-wide basis, some because it reflects their national and regional bargaining machinery and others because they have relatively small numbers of members in any particular college. It may make little sense to proliferate small Branches. This could provide a difficulty, however, if the staff represented in a county, city or borough branch now find that the local governing body of a college has far greater impact on pay and conditions than does the LEA. Plainly, there is no one model for organization, but all unions will address this further movement to local industrial relations activity.

In the case of the LEA college and adult education institute the potential for fragmentation of arrangements may be even greater than in the PCFC sector. The most important force for cohesion is likely to be the impracticality of governors handling mainstream employment issues in 700 different locations. Institutional heads who publicly strained at the bit in the past for greater autonomy were often those who turned to their town or county hall in private for decisions on the employment 'rules' because of the complexity of sailing single-handed. It would be complacent for a union to rely on this tendency to obey national rules, but unions will certainly find ways of encouraging it.

From an appreciation of the background to developments in industrial relations and an account of the changes in employment structures in post-school education, it becomes possible to detail the likely sources of conflict and the ways in which unions may respond.

From national to local bargaining

It has been noted that in the public sector most groups of employees have had pay and other conditions negotiated nationally, with arrangements in some sectors affected by regional bodies but all within national frameworks. Union negotiators pitch their principal arguments in terms of the salaries and conditions needed to attract, retain and motivate staff. Obviously the strongest case arises where it is most difficult to recruit, motivate and retain such staff because their pay and conditions have drifted farthest from the groups from which staff are to be drawn. There are no prizes for guessing that comparators based on the gap between public and private-sector pay in London will demonstrate a stronger case than could be shown in County Durham. This is a statement not of geographical hierarchy but of the rule of the market-place.

This simple reality is not, of course, unknown to the Government. It recognizes that if the national rate is driven by the requirements of the area in which the pay comparisons are most favourable for the unions' case, it then needs to break national rates into a number of local rates reflecting local market conditions. Thus, the Department of the Environment in particular has told public-sector employers that they should negotiate local rates. They argue that it is irresponsible to pay South-East rates to those who could be recruited for less. It would be disingenuous to believe that this had not crossed the minds of public-sector employers but traditionally they have prized the orderly relationship with unions that national arrangements provide.

All the pressure is now to break negotiation into local units. NATFHE has to some extent succeeded in resisting this trend, although the dangers are clear enough. If employers at the Government's behest are successful the very structure of career scales will come under threat when different regional 'rates for the job' emerge. Since a system of career scales is the accepted basis for career progression, the very substance of encouraging the migration of talent around the country without financial penalty and the professional character of employment is itself threatened. There is little point in Government or employers saying that talent can be encouraged to move by a competitive market structure. Colleges (and within them college libraries) cannot operate like competitive firms so long as their main, or 'core' business is education.

Whatever the threat, unions will adapt. It is well known that the local negotiation of salaries has become commonplace for private-sector unions, and many of them prefer it. The most effective unions have successfully exploited this route and will continue to do so as increasing shortages in skilled staff become more acute in the demographic downturn. Groups like lecturers and librarians will cope with the shift toward local bargaining, however lamentable from a professional point of view, by learning from both the successes and mistakes of other unions.

An immediate imperative will be to train local negotiators and arm them with detailed bargaining information on local market conditions. Indeed, this process is likely to benefit unions more generally because the more experienced and knowledgeable their membership, the more toughened by local activity, the greater will be the strength and capacity to deliver action of their national structures.

Some arguments will be available immediately to local negotiators. First, if the Government were right, employment would expand in low-wage/high-unemployment areas. The more wages can be depressed from national rates, the less unemployment there should be. Of course, the opposite is the case. Second, national pay bargaining is frequently preferred by employers since it typically sets a minimum rate which corresponds to the appropriate national level and safeguards employers from the confusion that always accompanies competitive undercutting. Indeed, since 1984 only about 35% of non-manual workers have had their pay increases determined by national bargaining. National deals in the private sector have tended to lead to pay levels generally set at the level the less successful employers can afford (i.e. a minimum rate) rather than to the premium rates in the South-East. Here again, the reality is the opposite of what the Government supposes it to be. National bargaining in the private sector does not generate high-pay levels. Local bargaining, on the other hand, tends to do so.

'Flexibility'
After the objective of breaking up national bargaining, the next most important element of employer and Government thinking is the fostering of what they call 'flexibility'. Both the use of Government agencies like the Mergers and Monopolies Commission for the unusual task of attacking 'restrictive practices' by unions, and the more common approach through bargaining (and stealth) on the part of employers have been strategies to accomplish two goals.

Many employers want their current workforce to do a wider variety of jobs and, in the public sector, to embrace the introduction of flexible job descriptions. This is equivalent to ending demarcation in the private sector. For teachers and lecturers this has meant the employers assuming the right to deploy staff for longer hours of teaching to cover for peaks at work and for absent colleagues. There is an employer attempt to blur the distinctions between teaching, preparation of courses, marking students' work, administration and so on. It is not difficult to find parallels in all branches of work in education. For example, other staff could be asked to work on an averaged annual contract rather than a contract with a weekly limit on hours. Librarians might be asked to use cataloguing and recording skills in other parts of the administration of colleges at times when the library is not as intensively used. Plainly, in the real world such periods are times when people catch up on backlogs of work and take their holidays but these sound arguments count for little with employers looking for flexibility.

Some unions have responded creatively to this kind of challenge by linking it to 'flexi-time' agreements for example, or encouraging the rotation of the more boring and low-skilled jobs. However, the potential for diluting professionalism creates its own problems. There will be structural conflict as a need for greater specialization at work rubs up against demands for dilution of skills and cost-efficiency.

Flexibility has come to mean other things for some employers. Some use it to describe flexible payment systems of a kind described earlier, namely a response to local market conditions. An increasingly common use of the term refers to numerical flexibility in the workforce, of having a small core of full-time staff and a larger number of part-time staff paid only when they are needed. The removal and reduction of rights in respect of unfair dismissal has made it easier to accomplish this. Part-time work is cheaper to employ for a number of reasons. The concept of the 'core firm', has emerged in the public sector. It is evident in many branches of public employment and the first major developments in this direction can now be seen in polytechnics. Employers aim to retain a group of full-time staff who combine some teaching with a band of middle-management administrative tasks, including responsibility for recruitment within a pool of casual, part-time lecturers. This pool is currently being created by offering early retirement to existing staff on tempting terms and then offering them part-time lecturing contracts without any administrative duties. Here again, it is not difficult to see the parallels between lecturers and other professional groups.

Unions will need to address this pressure for casualization so that they have an overall policy on the shedding of full-time staff. Employers with new powers, described above, will certainly want to learn successful tactics from each other and unions cannot rely on ad hoc responses.

Most of all, unions will want to assess the likely trajectory of these approaches. It would be prudent to plan in terms of the Government's secret report (November 1987) on civil service employment, which contains a public-sector blueprint. The report starts from a view that rather than regular patterns of employment, employees should be required to meet fluctuations in workload without a right to overtime pay. The model is instructive because it obviously has a wider potential for employers other than just those employing civil servants.

According to the report, all recruitment would be by open competition as is the case in education's professional grades. Among the factors judged on appointment would be 'promotability', and career advancement through grades would be by assessment and completion of approved training. All appointees would be recruited to a grade rather than a job and thus be open to undertaking any of a number of comparable jobs on that grade. Although there would be a normal retirement age, usually with an entitlement to a pension, it might be possible to employ individuals beyond that age.

To assist in these goals, there would be a concerted move to annualized hours contracts, recurring temporary contracts or contracts for fixed periods or tasks, and 'nil hours contracts' to engage staff to cover temporary shortages whilst avoiding accumulation of employment rights. There would be a massive increase in part-time employment and agreed homeworking.

These developments are all in the stealthy process of introduction in post-school education – they might almost have been the testbed. With each attempt to fracture the basis for reliable, career employment, comes a loss in the motivation of staff, an unwillingness to undergo training, and usually a loss of the very staff it is essential to retain. Their expertise migrates to other areas of employment. The drive to casualization inevitably reduces career opportunities for women first. It is doubtful that any gains in flexibility of work patterns can compensate.

Conclusion
In a difficult period, it is easier to catalogue the setbacks and to detail future problems than it is to provide consistent responses. Rhetorical rallying calls may appeal to the most active trade unionists but appear to have lost their charm among rank-and-file members. Indeed, many trade unionists and their unions have a concern for effective public policy-making, proper accountability in public services, and genuine efficiency in services provided.

However, the debate on accountability and efficiency has largely been hijacked by the Government, and there is a real difficulty in raising the issues within unions without appearing complicit in Government ideologies. This point is surely critical because, although it is easy enough to reiterate defensive tactics against pay cuts or adverse working patterns, defensiveness is not enough. It has not succeeded on its own in the last nine years nor will it now. Trade unions also need positive strategies to encounter new problems. They need to be able to turn circumstances to their advantage.

The battle against the break-up of national pay is important. Using all the arguments about the market for skilled occupations, taking full advantage of demographic trends, may well hurt entrepreneurial employers far more in this decade than in the last. Resistance to flexibility as conceived by central or local government is indispensable. Unionized staff need to take control of the working environment by developing new authoritative professional bodies and structures which support high standards and undiluted qualifications and thereby undermine Government objectives.

For lecturers, librarians and professional administrators, it is instructive to look at other professional groups. No doubt doctors, lawyers and accountants are under attack, but a betting person might not mind a wager on the likely outcome. Their control of their professional environment may be dented but its boundaries will not be significantly breached.

What provides this resilience is not just the prestige of these professions but sheer determination not to allow outside control of the professional qualification, membership, regulation and ethical systems. When teachers, lecturers, librarians and others learn to be as doggedly prescriptive, and take the same undiluted pride in the power of a high-quality professional system (not just what the profession does but its political authority over what it does), then they will have fortified their camp.

As it is, lecturers, librarians and others are too open, too generous. Perhaps they have too great a democratic regard for what others think and want of them. The 'service' ethic which is to be found in the ideology of most professional groups, has led to considerable self-effacement in post-school education. Of course, it is nice to be nice; at present it is also lethal.

References
1 Taylor, R., *The fifth estate: Britain's unions in the modern world*, rev. ed. London, Pan Books, 1980.
2 *Education Reform Act*, London, HMSO, 1988.

12 The GMB perspective *(Interview with John Edmonds)*

The GMB is an example of a union that has attempted to recognize and act on some of the changes which are affecting relationships, expectations and working conditions. It is, for example, providing a mechanism for women to be represented, to provide support for those in areas of work which were previously neglected and to shift ideologies and organizations to match to some extent the changing social shifts of the 1980s and 1990s.

The following provides a 'snapshot' of an organization in the process of change, and is the record of an interview with John Edmonds, General Secretary of the GMB.

The GMB perspective

Current developments must be seen in the context of major changes which are occurring in the country. Some of these have already been referred to as they are 'universal', but cannot be ignored in relation to GMB thinking and developments. The most important of these include the change in the structure of industry and the switch from manufacturing to service-based industries, as well as age-profile changes. Two other major elements are changes in the attitude towards work in general, as a way of life. There has been a move away from the 'protestant work ethic' and the concept that work provides a total 'personal' identity, towards the concept of part-time employment and temporary work being a perfectly acceptable way of living. In addition there has been an enormous increase in the number of women in the workforce, as a result of the many social and economic changes. Numerical increases have been matched by rising expectations of job satisfaction and conditions of work.

In this context of rapid change, the trade union movement can be seen to have its roots in an earlier and sociologically different scene and so it was in many ways the natural product of this scene. As with so many institutions, it developed ideologies and structures which related to a specific period, rather than for general future development. This meant that the movement was strong in large areas of industrial work and was in general male-dominated. These areas have changed rapidly during recent years and this change has been accelerated by the present government. This inevitable lack of synchronization between organization and environment has merely illustrated the inefficient organization of most unions, designed to carry out their tasks in a different climate at a different time.

Such changes highlighted the choices available to the movement in this decade. The crude choices were an inevitable decline, as has tended to happen in the United States, or a radical change in the structure and activities of unions. Such changes have been and are difficult to tackle in the current climate, as they are a contradiction to current legal and political activities and, of course, lack support from the ruling party.

The major themes of change which have to be faced by the union movement, and particularly the GMB, can be defined as:

Recruitment in the service industries
Recruitment in small-scale operations
Recruitment of women

These all interrelate and reinforce each other, and also lead into the other identified area of change, which is the recruitment of people for whom work is no longer the central identity-giving element in their lives, as indicated earlier.

No longer can and do the craft workers, for example, feel that the union is the centre of their working lives, as the number of women workers is rapidly being increased. Many women have children and/or elderly dependants and so do not necessarily devote all their lives to work, feeling that this is but one component of their lives. The union is concentrating on recruiting more women, in the context of increased flexibility of working patterns. Women are no longer being relegated to non-decision-making areas. As well as accommodating such changes, the union movement also has to recognize shifts in the atmosphere and ethos of workplaces, including a more flexible system of accountability and less rigid control, heightened by the increased use of new technology, where work is more concerned with tasks than with processes. If elements of rigidity are introduced into this changing atmosphere by the union movement and the structure of the organization, then this limits and inhibits both workers and managers, and so is now an unacceptable way of working. A current example of this is an embargo on overtime by a relatively strong union (AEU), imposing centralized conditions on its members, many of whom do not want this general policy to be implemented. They recognize its rigidity and do not want this. Members would much prefer an atmosphere of choice and flexibility, which reflects in the workplace the choices which they make for themselves and their families outside the workplace. It provides a more receptive environment and reduces tension.

The need for freer and more flexible organizations with advice and support to members of those organizations, becomes more and more apparent, and diversity is welcomed, rather than an ever-increasing bureaucracy. This diversity is reflected by different lifestyles and personal objectives of individuals and the need for support mechanisms to function in places of work. It is linked to a move away from paternalism and maternalism towards advice and information, adding to the quality of life. Informed advice is increasingly important in a complex world, but still a world which in many cases does allow the individual to choose his or her place of work and so in which centralized wage negotiations are increasingly remote – flexibility allows many people to leave employment if conditions are not acceptable. Those workers who are constrained need more and more support from the union movement, but support for *them*, rather than a constraining set of conditions. This highlights the shift in trade union roles and the movement away from seeing the function of the movement as a simple opposition fighting with employers, perceived as the enemy in organization terms, to the new and emergent role of support and help for members. These shifts in perception mirror the unconscious ways in which individuals perceive organizations and project their own feelings onto individuals and groups, as outlined earlier in the book.

Within the GMB there has been a concentrated move to follow these social and economic changes with changes in union philosophy. These radical ideas, in development terms, include work on current employment patterns, so that an informed analysis can be used to affect the future of the union. These changes have been analysed and considered region by region and particularly in areas where recruitment appears to be potentially good. This process may involve the amalgamating of smaller but potential recruitment bases, and concentration on areas which tend to be excluded from the movement. These include the retail trades and hotel and catering trades, for example, who include many part-time and female workers, but who as a workforce could considerably widen the organizational base of the union.

Once these target areas and workers have been identified, then analysis should begin to be concerned with their needs. Gender issues are clearly important and from the Union's perspective, it is important that the considerable number of women members (30% of the membership), should have those needs met. The 'system' itself may not be conducive to full participation, as it is male-dominated and male-organized, and so a system of reserved seats on the Executive has been formulated, plus ten extra seats for women. It is hoped that this will accelerate the natural process of women moving into positions within the union, reflecting their numerical strength. A balanced Executive will then, hopefully, begin to reflect a wider range of views and opinions.

These changes must also percolate through the hierarchy, so that Branches and activists are equally aware of the need for women to have a stronger say in the affairs of the union and are not the victims of overt or covert discrimination. To try and combat this, each Branch now has a Branch Equality Officer, to strengthen this equal rights policy. To support this further, there is a need for training opportunities to be provided for women, but in a context and atmosphere in which they feel supported and able to participate.

Women's workplace projects have been designed and set up to train activists to become representatives. This is a slow and time-consuming process, but crucial to the development of the organization and a clear indication of the wish to involve women in the atmosphere of change. The number of women members is steadily increasing as a result of union response to this constituency.

The 'image' of the union, previously very male and macho, stemming from the male- and craft-dominated workplace ethos, has also been considered. Publications are now produced with considerable care, a badge with a corporate image has been produced, indicating not just an image but a philosophy behind the image. This includes joint efforts to improve areas such as health and safety, not through confrontation but through cooperation. This is a positive move away from previous images and a conscious effort to face the world in a realistic way.

If members are to be treated with care and support, then services also have to be designed for them. The current computerized membership list has been used to improve communication, so that information is fed directly to individuals, rather than through Branch officers. Linked with this have been packages negotiated with banks and other organizations, again to improve the quality of life of individual members.

A recent initiative on education and training has also been launched and the ideas are contained in the document entitled *The 1990s and beyond*. This includes identifying training needs, setting targets, organizing resources and evaluating programmes. The training and education programme will support the recruitment policies outlined above and link up with other areas of GMB development.

This concentration on a common identity, the needs of women in employment and in specific areas of employment, plus a general concern for recruitment, are all indications of a change of direction. However, all large organizations, and the GMB is no exception, are slow to change and this is a long-term process. It involves changes in attitudes, and these are notoriously slow to effect. Those already in membership and often in areas of industry dominated by white male workers, are being asked to change on behalf of a whole new range of potential workers, in acute need of help in many cases. They are represented by part-time women workers in retail, hotel and cleaning industries. So the traditional hard-core workers are being asked to change for the potential of the future – a very difficult task to achieve in terms of human faith and goodwill. Balance and understanding are easy to write and speak about, but not so easy to effect.

References
1 GMB., *The 1990's and beyond*, London, Fontana/Collins, 1987.

Further reading
Gill, D. and Ungerson, B., *Equal pay – the challenge of equal value*, London, Institute of Personnel Management, 1984.
Trade unions and their members, London, HMSO, 1988 (Green paper).
Trades Union Congress, *Images of inequality*, London, TUC, 1984.

13 Introduction to the viewpoints of practitioners   Rosemary Raddon

The interviews must be seen in the current social setting and in relation to political changes and ideologies. These ideologies influence the policies, practices and organization of local government, and in turn the dynamics within organizations. Interpersonal and industrial relations tensions then respond, change or crystallize in opposition.

The political backcloth is a crucial part of any consideration of personal relationships in the workplace. The structures and systems which now are integrated into local authorities and which surround recruitment, disputes, tribunals, legislation, job descriptions and pay are also a vital element. These form a system of protecting personnel, as well as employers, against exploitation and provide an operational and organizational framework. This framework grew and developed side-by-side with the moves in the private sector towards performance indicators and performance-related pay, in a climate of 'managers must manage'. In some ways these two strands interlink and support each other, and each borrows from the other as value-for-money and privatization moves increase. It would be simplistic to argue that these developments represent political ideologies of left and right, but in terms of local government, tensions exist between what are perceived to be the interests of the communities, constituencies or client groups which the major parties represent while in power, and ideological ways of supporting these interests through differing styles of service delivery.

The interrelationship of party politics of either political persuasion with the local workforce has also reflected these shifts. Many political ideas are now mirrored, for example, in conditions of service, participative management, hierarchical or broad-based structures and other managerial philosophies at a local level. Issues such as harmonization and the consideration of inherent racist and sexist attitudes to staff, within organizations and in relation to recruitment policies, are also examples of the ways in which practices and perceptions, social change and managerial responsiveness overlap and interlink. Member and officer relationships are elements which are also illustrated. Again, recent events in the restructuring of large authorities in relation to library and information services, can be seen as an example of political initiatives producing service changes. Both interviews are thumbnail sketches only, but indicate alterations in politics, perceptions and ideologies. These in turn are reflected in personal relationships and organizational change. The interviews represent an overview from both sides of the political spectrum, and so solutions and ideas as well as ideology reflect the political underpinning. Both authorities have reacted and are reacting in quite different ways to trade union policies and industrial relations. Both are concerned with the provision of services, and so together can symbolize the concerns and solutions which they have adopted. They reflect in some way all of the issues raised in earlier sections of the book.

In the London Borough of Wandsworth (Tory controlled in 1990), libraries function under the broad umbrella of 'Leisure'. It is necessary to understand the way in which the Leisure Directorate functions to appreciate the ways in which the libraries function. The first interview gives that broad overview, in the context of change.

The second interview, a perception of industrial relations, is given by the former Chief Officer of a large left-wing metropolitan authority and previously of a London Borough. It reflects the difficulties and tensions which provoke and fuel industrial relations in such a setting, and, equally important, analyses the reasons for these. It complements the interview from Wandsworth, in that the political viewpoint is at the other end of the political spectrum, and so shows why in one authority there is very little industrial unrest, and why there is considerable unrest in the other. It also illustrates the reasons for the continuation of this unrest, and why many management theories and practices fail to produce an effective working environment unless the political underpinning is clearly understood. People at work are at the centre of change, and cannot operate in isolation from change.

References
Local Government and Housing Act, London, HMSO, 1989.
'Cambridge: another reorganisation, another non-librarian', *Library Association record*, **92** (12), 879.

14 Viewpoints of practitioners

14.1 London Borough of Wandsworth

14.1.1 *The employers' perspective: an overview*
Interview with Lance Garrett, Director of Amenity Services

In general terms there have been enormous changes in the Borough during the past ten years, more probably than in the previous fifty. Current practices must be seen within this context and also in relation to those factors outlined in the introduction.

The main developments have been concerned with the passing of the Education Reform Act, competitive contract tendering and the privatization of some services. One of the major aspects of the Act was the abolition of the Inner London Education Authority (ILEA), thereby passing responsibility for education to individual inner London boroughs. Improved but localized financial management of schools, in the climate of accountability, was another result of the Act. This local management of schools, plus the challenge of information technology were two major planks in the Borough's planning. The appointment of a Director of Education and an education plan provided a base for these changes. At the same time the Borough had to weld together, through collective bargaining, groups of people involved in education, but who had previously been employed on a variety of salary scales and conditions of service. So these groups, through collective bargaining, have become part of the Borough's workforce and adopted Wandsworth's conditions of service. Further changes may include the introduction of a four-term year to utilize staff and plant at a maximum level. Assessment techniques will also be an element in performance criteria in the educational field.

Privatization has presented another challenge to the Borough. Street cleansing was the first major service involved, which has been a frequent area of major inter-personal and inter-union disputes in local government. The privatization of street cleaning started in 1982, followed by refuse collection, and other services, some of which are now being re-tendered. These include conveniences, library cleaning, halls cleaning, housing estates cleaning and attending to old people's homes.

Budgetary constraints are, of course, linked to the touchstone of the rates. In 1978 Wandsworth was very highly rated, but now, under a Tory administration, Wandsworth has the lowest community charge and the largest population of the inner London Boroughs. Details of the population profile need to be compared to those of other London Boroughs for true comparisons to be made. (See figure 14.1).

92   People and work

B4.0'4/88

Table 26   Household projections for London local authorities

Thousands

Area	1981	1986 Low	1986 High	1991 Low	1991 High	1996 Low	1996 High	2001 Low	2001 High
	(1)	(2)	(3)	(4)	(5)	(6)	(7)	(8)	(9)
City of London	2.4	2.1	2.1	2.1	2.1	2.0	2.1	2.0	2.1
Barking and Dagenham	57.0	56.4	56.4	57.3	57.5	58.2	58.7	59.0	59.7
Barnet	110.6	114.3	114.3	116.1	117.2	117.6	119.7	119.2	122.1
Bexley	79.3	82.1	82.1	85.2	85.6	85.4	86.3	85.2	86.6
Brent	93.0	97.1	97.1	98.6	99.5	99.3	101.0	100.0	102.4
Bromley	112.6	115.0	115.0	118.1	118.8	120.2	121.7	121.8	123.9
Camden	78.2	81.1	81.1	83.0	84.1	84.3	86.2	85.5	88.2
Croydon	118.8	121.2	121.2	124.5	125.3	127.9	129.6	130.7	133.1
Ealing	104.7	112.5	112.5	114.7	115.6	115.0	116.8	115.6	118.2
Enfield	97.9	99.7	99.7	101.6	102.2	102.1	103.2	102.1	103.9
Greenwich	80.9	82.7	82.7	85.0	85.5	87.9	88.8	90.3	91.7
Hackney	73.5	76.1	76.1	77.5	78.1	77.3	78.5	77.5	79.3
Hammersmith and Fulham	66.3	66.6	66.6	67.5	68.3	67.7	69.1	68.3	70.3
Haringey	82.8	79.7	79.7	81.0	81.8	81.7	83.2	82.5	84.6
Harrow	72.9	74.5	74.5	76.1	76.7	77.6	78.7	78.7	80.3
Havering	86.2	87.5	87.5	88.6	89.2	89.0	90.1	88.5	90.1
Hillingdon	83.9	85.7	85.7	88.9	89.5	90.1	91.4	90.8	92.7
Hounslow	75.6	77.5	77.5	79.8	80.4	81.3	82.6	82.6	84.4
Islington	69.0	69.1	69.1	70.6	71.2	70.5	71.8	71.0	72.8
Kensington and Chelsea	65.6	65.3	65.3	64.1	65.3	63.2	65.2	63.1	65.6
Kingston upon Thames	53.5	53.8	53.8	55.1	55.5	55.4	56.4	55.8	57.1
Lambeth	103.3	102.0	102.0	102.7	103.8	102.9	104.9	103.6	106.4
Lewisham	94.1	93.7	93.7	97.0	97.6	99.0	100.1	100.7	102.5
Merton	66.2	67.5	67.5	69.1	69.5	69.9	70.8	70.7	72.1
Newham	78.8	76.8	76.8	82.7	83.1	87.1	87.9	90.9	92.2
Redbridge	85.3	86.8	86.8	90.2	89.0	93.3	90.9	95.7	92.4
Richmond upon Thames	67.2	69.6	69.6	70.1	70.8	70.6	71.8	71.2	73.0
Southwark	89.1	89.3	89.3	93.9	94.4	96.1	97.2	98.2	99.8
Sutton	65.4	67.0	67.0	68.2	68.7	69.3	70.2	70.3	71.6
Tower Hamlets	56.7	58.5	58.5	61.3	61.6	62.7	63.4	64.3	65.5
Waltham Forest	82.8	83.1	83.1	84.1	84.6	85.2	86.3	86.3	87.8
Wandsworth	106.1	107.3	107.3	108.4	109.3	107.8	109.8	108.1	110.9
Westminster, City of	83.9	78.0	78.0	80.2	81.4	81.7	83.9	82.9	85.8
Inner London	969.1	971.7	971.7	993.2	1,002.7	1,003.1	1,021.1	1,015.5	1,040.9
Outer London	1,674.4	1,707.9	1,707.9	1,750.1	1,760.4	1,776.1	1,797.1	1,797.5	1,828.2
Group A boroughs	1,049.8	1,045.5	1,045.5	1,072.0	1,082.1	1,083.9	1,103.3	1,098.6	1,126.0
Group B boroughs	1,593.7	1,634.1	1,634.1	1,671.4	1,681.0	1,695.3	1,714.8	1,714.4	1,743.1
Greater London	2,643.5	2,679.6	2,679.6	2,743.3	2,763.1	2,779.2	2,818.2	2,813.1	2,869.1

Source: London Research Centre

Note: The low figures are derived from high net migration loss projections - see Table 24, B and D. The High figures are consistent with dwelling stock changes between 1986 and 1996 and are equivalent to the low net migration loss projections - see Table 24, A and C.

Reproduced by kind permission of The London Research Centre (1987–88), Annual Abstract of Greater London Statistics

Fig. 14.1   Household projections for Local local authorities

So currently Wandsworth is in the position of focussing on the services which are provided, and making decisions on the structure of these and on the allocation of resources. The staffing element has been crucial in this process. There are now seven Directorates, including Education, staff have been redeployed, but within the white-collar staffing areas there has been a policy of no compulsory redundancies. (This has not applied to the manual unions.) Personal salaries are maintained in redeployment, but not necessarily status. As services and directorates were reorganized, other staff and services were absorbed into Wandsworth, as a result of the abolition of the GLC. Education is an area where staff were and will be rationalized, and the process has been accelerated by the abolition of the ILEA. The same process applied to those staff previously employed by the GLC, so that conditions of service were consistent throughout the Borough.

During the period of rationalizing services in the early 1980s, white-collar workers were willing to be fully involved in these discussions, although some older members of staff disliked the new regime and moved to jobs elsewhere. Since the finalizing of the directorate structure, work has continued on improving conditions of service, such as health and safety issues, filling posts within an agreed timescale and improving the consultation process.

The consultation process at Member level consists of the joint staff negotiating committee (including six Members) with a negotiating sub-committee for specific issues. At departmental level there are joint consultative committees, which, in the case of the Leisure Directorate, include leisure management, representatives from the shop stewards within the union and staff-side representatives. (A separate negotiating process and machinery exists for the manual workers.) An interesting point emerges here over the low key and limited amount of involvement in the negotiating process by most staff. This may indicate excellent conditions of service, a desire not to maintain a high profile with management, inertia, or an inclination to concentrate on career moves in a competitive climate.

It is generally considered that disputes over terms and conditions of service and restructuring and reorganization have been resolved. There still remains an effective process for grievances, formally through the committee structures to the Whitley Council and informally through the Director. The formal processes are used infrequently.

Re-assessing services, maintaining those which are statutory, while reviewing those of long standing, plus income derived from increasing the use of facilities, the selling of surplus land and council house sales, has led to Wandsworth's position as that with the lowest community charge and yet highest capital spender in the London area.

Services have been considered using criteria such as efficiency, cost, new technological applications and the need to train staff in customer care. Privatization of some services has been the end-result of these deliberations, particularly the refuse and cleaning services. Training has been carried out in-house as well as by external agencies such as the Industrial Society. Other areas of training reflect the ethos of the Borough. They include training in poor performance procedures, the disciplinary code, report writing, meeting the public, telephone answering techniques, race awareness and recruitment procedures as well as marketing techniques. In the area of Leisure, including libraries, services have to be competitive, as they are not demand-led, as in social services or housing.

The political background to these moves prior to 1989 was that of a radical left-wing council, succeeded by a Tory council. Currently, the traditional weapons of interpersonal relationships, that is the strike and work to rule, have little strength, as the threat used in return by the Council is to remove the compulsory no-redundancy policy. The Borough has a history of few industrial disputes in the areas staffed by white-collar workers, partly because of these relatively good relationships. There has been more unrest among the manual workers (again to be seen in relation to the changes outlined earlier) and this tension has led to the privatization of the refuse services. Other areas of privatization, as mentioned earlier, have followed – cleaning, attendance in homes and cleaning of housing estates. The contract for the privatization of the meals service to the elderly was terminated, as the service provided was not of a sufficiently high standard and the 'quality' of care was not being maintained – a performance indicator that led to an immediate change in policy.

In general terms relationships between staff and management are reasonable and the consultative machinery is felt to be adequate. There are checks and balances, for example the 10 days' notice given to the union, prior to publication of committee reports, so that full consultation can take place. The ethos is that managers should and must manage and that staff must perform – performance indicators will be used as from 1 April 1990. This ethos links to that of an effective marketing concept, with the minimum of Member involvement in direct service delivery. The marketing ethos and the need to generate income necessitates the customer-care training and the encouragement of an increase in use of services, rather than constant increases in charges. Marketing in the commercially accepted sense of the word, segmentation benefits, the exchange concept, and costs are valid and important.

Issues which have been labelled as a cause of tension and strain among professionals, arising from privatization, have not yet surfaced in Wandsworth. In some parts of the country, in areas such as housing, architecture and management, professionals previously employed in the public sector have moved into the private sector – they have then been employed as consultants working with erstwhile employees in the public sector. These new sets of relationship may cause tensions in the workforce as a direct result of political initiatives and are an indication of potential unease but also creativity.

Future developments
Staff and personnel relations will be concerned with the implementation of effective service delivery and this will include the implementation of performance related pay. This will provide one clear criterion for rewarding the achievement of objectives which have been firmly defined in political and service terms. A pilot project has already been established for middle management. Incentive schemes are also being implemented to improve productivity and new contracts issued with performance related pay. Performance related pay schemes will cover specific qualitative aspects of work above senior management level, but will concentrate on quantitative aspects of work for staff below senior management level. (It is easier to measure productivity in terms of plants grown, streets swept, etc.) Bonus elements will be paid under the umbrella of competitive contract tendering and this structure will be particularly evident in the tendering of schemes for Battersea Park (previously under the aegis of the GLC). Economic realism and the need for competitive pricing are seen by many workers as valid arguments. These agreements have been worked out at district and local level and were preferred by the manual workers to redundancy pay. Competitive contract tendering is a more contentious issue in the area of Leisure, as there are fewer agencies with the necessary expertise in the care of parks, for example, who are able to make these tenders.

Wandsworth's policies can be summed up as working towards cost-effective services. Involvement in services which are seen as appropriate to the local government machinery, such as education, are acceptable, but others which may be more effectively carried out by private-sector agencies are not seen to be the prerogative of local government, regardless of their interaction with the local community.

14.1.2 The employees' perspective: an overview
Interview with John Hall, Staff-side Secretary, NALGO

The reverse side of this case study reflects the perspective of the white-collar union, represented by a full-time staff-side secretary. An important element to note is that the post is full-time, funded by the Borough, and is supported with accommodation and clerical help. (A parallel post exists for the manual, or blue-collar, section.) The existence of these posts, responsible to the union body but embedded in the formal negotiating machinery, legitimizes the machinery, but also enables it to be used creatively and in an ad hoc way.

The union perspective of industrial and interpersonal relationships in the Borough must be seen in the context of local recent political developments. The period of expansion under a Labour-controlled council during the 1960s and early 1970s was marked by concern for job security and full employment. Towards the end of the 1970s there was a radical change, and the council became Tory controlled. Policies of reductions in staff and services introduced a more complex and difficult period of workplace relationships. These in turn generated strains on the workforce and so on the unions, who were required to protect their members' interests in a changing industrial-relations climate.

In 1979/80 local unions were involved in a 'think tank' exercise in the Borough, focusing on the need to protect staff employed in the Town Hall, and to produce a policy. This would be based on the assumption that any compulsory redundancies or loss of earnings would be fought, and that initiatives and policies should be Member-led. A policy was evolved that was based on the concept of no redundancies, but linked to one of restricted recruitment and internal reorganization. Behind this was the philosophy of an efficient and smaller workforce. When privatization policies began to be implemented at a later date, there were few radical changes in the internal organization of the Borough.

In line with national political trends, the Council gradually became more right-wing in its thinking, with a promise of no rate (community charge) increases for the electorate as one of its many political planks. This implicitly suggested that some reductions in services or staff would be necessary. The workforce reacted violently against this possibility, which not only threatened job security, but also reneged on earlier promises. Their fears were further fuelled by projected figures of 700 redundancies. Industrial action was the inevitable result. A strike fund had already been established (6% of union dues), and a mass meeting challenged the threatened redundancies, breaking earlier agreements. The resultant industrial action was planned to affect the internal mechanisms of the Council, rather than hurt ratepayers through direct action against services, such as housing or social services. Communications, transport and the servicing of committees were three major areas. The political response was to suggest early-retirement and voluntary-severance schemes as a possible way of reducing the workforce. Meetings between elected Members and union representatives evolved a negotiated compromise which was based on reorganization and voluntary severance. The union accepted this, with the proviso that any implementation of redundancy would result in industrial action.

The next change involved the privatization of refuse and street-cleaning services, producing a different set of tensions with different results. Opposition to these policies was mounted, in collaboration with the manual workers' union, and a large rally voted for industrial action in support of the manual workers, and against these policies. The industrial action, however, eventually collapsed and the elected Members refused to participate in any negotiations. Union members had been advised to enter into negotiations with the Council but refused, and as the industrial action collapsed, privatization policies were implemented. The white collar unions are now the major negotiating force, due to redundancies and declining numbers among the manual workers. The key issue of no redundancies is still the basic plank for negotiations.

Running parallel with the change in the power of the manual or blue collar workers has been the maintenance in the Borough of an efficient and cost effective, although small, direct labour force. In the arena of competitive tendering, it has been able to tender on equal or better terms with the commercial sector. In one area, the delivery of meals to elderly people, it has taken over from a commercial contractor, whose services were terminated due to unacceptable standards of service delivery in a sensitive area.

The next major issue, following national legislation, will be that of tendering and privatization in the Leisure sector. The development of Battersea Park, either in-house or by the private sector, will be watched with interest by other Boroughs elsewhere in the country.

At the same time, negotiations have been proceeding over conditions of service for staff leaving the abolished ILEA and joining the Borough. There is a need for some kind of unified conditions of service, without a great reduction in benefits. These negotiations peaked in 1990 when the transfer of staff from the ILEA to the Boroughs was finalized. The community charge was implemented in the same year, linked to the need to provide education on a

Borough-wide, not capital-wide, basis. Also being implemented were pilot schemes concerned with performance-related pay. Pilot recruitment and retention schemes were also being examined.

The general atmosphere of Member/union relationships in the Borough has been relaxed, and both sides want to avoid extreme tensions. The union is anxious to protect its members, but needs to do so in a rapidly changing political climate, backed by far-reaching legislation and changes in social concepts. Stable relationships may be difficult to maintain. It faces a difficult task, and has to balance the needs of its members against a clear demand for improved services, in a climate of economic effectiveness. The concepts of protection and the provision of jobs within a socialist framework are no longer valid. But there is an equally clear need to maintain the existing relationships and negotiating machinery as protective measures.

14.2 Politics and practitioners
Interview with a Director of Housing

Historically, as a result of the London reorganization of 1965, followed by the establishment of fewer but larger local authorities stemming from this, active trade unionism built around the large county boroughs, then rapidly extended itself by networking through the new large authorities. So by the mid-1970s, hierarchical, structural trade unionism had come to stay within local government and the agendas for trade union action were increasingly informed by the political characteristics of the administrations now controlling the local authorities.

It is believed that general support for local government trade unions developed out of trade union intervention in defence of employees' rights and job opportunities at the time of local government reorganization in the 1960s and early 1970s. Subsequently, this popular support was increasingly called upon to underpin the pursuit of wider issues. By 1975, however, the preparedness of local authority staff in general to demand negotiations and even support conflict strategies including strike action had greatly increased as had the appreciation by local authority staff of the need for reciprocal solidarity with other public-sector workers. This related to major organizational change in structures such as the Health Service.

These new staff attitudes and trade-union arrangements were well established by the time the Conservative Government came into office in 1979 and the subsequent development of trade unionism within local authorities was informed by the progressive revelation of the Conservative Party's intention to demunicipalize and privatize local authority and other public sector services.

To summarize, the circumstances of recent history which inform the current industrial relations situation in local authorities has four identifiable stages:

1 The transition from conservatism to issue-based trade unionism built particularly upon awareness of health and safety issues at the office workplace
2 Trade union advocacy at a time of local government reorganization, generating staff loyalty and support
3 The development of structuralism and the replication of the bureaucratic framework
4 Consolidation created by external threat, defence strategies and aggressive 'fightback'.

Trade unions, politicians and the consumer
Local government is a matrix in which three interests have to be accommodated: those of the politicians, the professionals (workers) and the people. Often the charge has been laid that local government serves its professionals more than its politicians and certainly more than it serves the people.

In Britain in the 1970s, the left wing of the Labour Party, identifying the conservatism of local government officers as resistance to the implementation of socialist policies and programmes, attempted to challenge this commonly held view by breaking the power of the large local authority departments. The initial assault was followed by the subjection of local government officers to much closer political scrutiny and direction than they had received hitherto.

Ostensibly this attack on the officer power-base was proclaimed as necessary in order to make services more responsive and accountable to the population at large (the electors). In particular, in the major cities, it became an assault primarily on the Housing and Public Works Departments within which vast power and resources had been concentrated in immediate post-war reconstruction and in the implementation of the slum clearance and redevelopment programmes of the 1950s and 1960s. Their officer power-bases had, by and large, been further extended and consolidated as a result of the centralizing and municipal-massing process of 1974 reorganization. The reforming politicians' assault, motivated often by resentment at the imposition of comprehensive redevelopment, was vigorously resisted by the traditionalist 'city fathers' and 'boss politicians' of their own as well as other parties (whose reputations were also at stake), and was impeded by the often devious resourcefulness of Chief and Senior Officers as they mobilized and subsequently organized to defend the status quo.

In order to further their ambition of securing a grip on the reins of power, left-wing Labour Party politicians built alliances with the increasingly powerful workplace trade unions in the hope of opening up a second front and undermining the foundations of Chief Officers' departmental power-bases. By this means they hoped to take control of the bureaucracy by neutralizing the authority of the departmental heads. Here and there, by a combination of popular campaigns, e.g. against slum clearance, and by exposing maladministration and the cosy relationships which existed between Chief Officers and 'boss politicians', the top-down power structures and decision-making framework of certain local authorities were shaken and, in some cases, shattered (notably the London Boroughs).

However, once the traditional hierarchy had been weakened, Chief Officer power questioned and revolt in the ranks given the seal of political approval, the imminent collapse into anarchy could be kept at bay only by more and more Elected Member intervention and direct control. This, though, is but one of the outcomes of the political assault on the traditional officer power-base and must be considered alongside several other strands of post-war social and political development which have impacted upon local government, and which contribute to the industrial-relations environment.

At the start of the 1970s the national rent strike associated with the Housing Finance Bill unlocked a considerable amount of working-class activity and organization and though, in the years immediately following, high-profile community action subsided somewhat, the vestigial remains of local organization survived to be mobilized later around other issues. In some cases community groups had been assisted if not manipulated by young 'politicos' parachuted into sites of community conflict much as they were parachuted into industrial-conflict situations elsewhere.

The subsequent growth in power and influence of ward Labour parties in the major conurbations owes much to such extreme left wing infiltration which paralleled, and indeed reinforced, the activities of reforming Labour Councillors, who on the one hand were confronting the local government power structures, whilst on the other having to demonstrate their personal political purity to local party members.

Such politicians, whilst recognizing the need for informed centralized decision-making, sought to avoid the label 'boss politician' and attempted through the caucus and the executive structures of the party to achieve collective decision-making. The various Labour Party forums which offered informal access to the trade unions became obvious lobbying locations where the workers' case could be put and where Elected Members could be mandated to deliver a decision supportive of the workers. Industrial relations thus formed a political party/trade union axis, working against existing Chief Officer power bases.

Meanwhile 'management' in the persons of Chief and Senior Officers, frequently oblivious to this network, still believed they were free to negotiate on behalf of their local authorities with trade unions and community groups, remitting for Member approval at the termination of negotiations the outcome of those negotiations. They soon came to realize how naïve they had been. So it was that increasingly in the 1970s Elected Members not only reduced management's scope for independent professional and managerial action on behalf of their local authorities, but also participated in negotiations themselves directly with the trade unions. This was a crucial development in industrial relations.

This muddying of the traditional waters left many managers perplexed and often feeling impotent in the teeth of what in their view were simple management/trade union issues which could easily be handled within 'due process'. In many authorities, standing orders were silent on this issue and the various local codes for interpretation in the *Purple book* were extremely thin when compared with the *Green book* arrangements for manual-workers' negotiations. It is for this reason, it is believed, that the Elected Members' intrusion into the industrial-relations area made its first appearance in connection with white-collar workers rather than blue-collar workers. Throughout the 1970s, however, and more recently with increasing areas of privatization, close Member involvement in manual workers' negotiations has also become an important feature of the conduct of business in the local authority workplace.

Rewards and opportunities

Before 1974, when there were three times the current number of local authorities, rewards for local-government officers were largely incremental pay, career progression within a particular local authority, or career progression by movement between local authorities. This scope for securing responsibility, for exercising choice, obtaining variety in work experience and opportunities for job enlargement was greatly reduced following 1974. When the new local authorities had been staffed there was, for the next few years, limited opportunity for career progression, and many a young ambitious graduate, frustrated by what appeared to be a suffocating hierarchy, pursued opportunities for demonstrating her/his creativity and communication skills within the trade-union organization rather than the departmental organization.

Such trade-union involvement gave these officers opportunities to manipulate and control the sections in which they worked. Whilst they clearly did not receive the rewards associated with being a section head, they did not on the other hand carry any line-management responsibilities nor have to deal with such consequences as affected the organization or their colleagues. The loop from shop steward to Elected Member gave Councillors the ammunition they required to criticize Chief Officers and undermine their prestige and self-esteem, by demonstrating superior though biased operational knowledge from the coalface of the department. In this way, front-line supervision – the bedrock of any organization – was also undermined and placed as hostage within the framework of the trade-union organization. At this point, and egged on by these frustrated would-be middle managers, the trade unions applied themselves to every single detail of the conduct of the organization's business, challenging with hard information and with the benefit of insider knowledge, every management decision on the basis that it was a 'trade-union issue'.

New technology par excellence illustrates this trend and particularly the tendency for those workers who in different circumstances would have been the enthusiastic developers of organizational change in managerial positions, and whose background, knowledge and skill fitted them for that purpose, to become in many cases the mainstays of the resistance to change.

It is ironic that when these officers finally pursued promotion the trade-union organization within which they achieved recognition and to which they gave their loyalty subsequently accused them of 'selling out' their comrades. Thus, backed into a corner, many declined career development or simply left the local authorities' employment. Those who remained often resented the peer-group pressure which prevented them from realizing their potential. 'Traditional' 1960s municipal values were thus eroded.

In such workplaces, discipline, programming and planning is currently extremely hard to sustain and requires the most resilient, tenacious and pugnacious of managers to achieve results. It also means for serious task-centred and target-oriented managers frequent confrontation with the centres of political power. Little wonder then that the turnover of Chief Officers in local government has increased so rapidly and that staff turnover is currently so high.

The intractable web of professional, political trade-union responses to issues of change has been seen at its worst in the London Boroughs and in metropolitan districts. Such difficulties are of course additional to the inevitably increasing complexities of local government administration over a period of rapid technological change and when municipal organizations in general have also been subjected to an ideological attack by central government. The difficulties of the last 10 years have simply compounded those which were apparent in the studies undertaken prior to reorganization in 1974 and which, it was believed, could be addressed by the institution of a corporate management framework.

Whilst some local authorities seriously set about establishing a corporate framework, many were confronted by the problem of connecting political decision-making to professional execution of political requirements. The structural symmetry necessitated through the corporate approach required that departments were matched by committees and that boundary definition was tightly adhered to. To apply this in a complex political framework created considerable tension.

On the one hand the requirements of sensible management suggested a reduction in the number of departments from upwards of 15 to fewer than 8. On the other hand, political realism and the needs of caucus and cabal required an ever-increasing number of committees, subcommittees, panels and working parties to feed the process of political patronage. The requirements of patronage were, of course, in addition to the quite natural tendency for the majority of Elected Members to wish to participate in the largest number of forums where they could (a) find out what was going on and (b) articulate, as advocates, the needs of their wards and constituents. Even where, despite these pressures, local authorities managed in the early stages to get their corporate act together, it was not long before the thin veil of corporate order became transparent, and tensions in the workplace were clear.

The tendency of trade unions to develop a structure which reflects the power structure of management has already been referred to. However, the trade unions never achieved a corporate approach, as this managerial phenomena was already in decline by the time they attempted to formulate a collective approach. Officers' internecine warfare was paralleled by similar conflict between different trade-union interests and the best the trade unions achieved in any particular local authority was a Joint Staffs and Joint Works Committee apparatus.

Trade union inter-relationships are complex and in most local authorities cannot be easily disentangled from local Labour Party machinery. The major local authority trade unions affiliated to the Labour Party are the G & M, the T & G and NUPE. Whilst essentially blue-collar trade unions, they each have white-collar divisions: MATSA, ACTS and NUPE (Officers) respectively. In addition, the various direct labour organizations within local authorities have the whole range of engineering and construction trade union representation, of which the most influential is UCATT. NALGO, of course, is a trade union *not* affiliated to the Labour Party and is therefore unable directly to deploy delegates into local Labour Party machinery.

The affiliated trade unions enjoy varying degrees of influence within local Labour parties and since the present Government's drive against trade unions, with the corresponding reduction in national membership, and its broad-based attack on local government, many of the tensions and confusions have arisen because of the conflict between individual trade union needs and maintaining the wider defence of the employment environment. Whilst outside local government the resistance of some trade unions to change has been broken by other trade unions entering into single-union agreements with employers within local government, cross-union poaching, supposedly prevented by the Bridlington Agreement, has been extensive and the resulting mutual suspicion has tended to undermine solidarity.

A further tendency which is worthy of comment is the manifestation of apparent industrial relations issues caused by conflict, not so much between trade unions, but between left-wing factions inside and outside the Labour Party, who shift their trade union allegiance for political tactical advantage. Disputes and direct action often emerge as a result of one faction trying to demonstrate to the workforce in general that it has more machismo than the other faction.

These then are the major trends, tendencies, forces, interests and factions which together form the culture in which Senior Officers must apply their management skill to deal with the industrial relations aspects of human resources management.

The local-government managers' response

Quite often to their cost, Senior Officers have applied their repertoire of problem-solving skills to the industrial relations issues with which they are presented, only to find that the predictability of their behaviour has been relied on to create a springboard from which a small and local issue is projected onto a wider platform where it becomes a major dispute. At that point the application of damage-control techniques will not necessarily rescue the situation since they may also have been relied upon by the initiators of the action to demonstrate a general managerial weakness and tendency towards conciliation.

On the other hand, management escalation by summary disciplinaries and sackings, far from resolving the problem and restoring order, may be blocked by a lack of political 'bottle' or wisdom, where the political administration perceives that the aim of the activists is to show how insensitive, Thatcherite, Stalinist (or whatever) the political/officer leadership really is. Chief Officers who create such difficulties for political administrations seldom last long.

Chief Officers in such situations are unlikely to find solutions, success or survival, therefore, by the well-meaning application of management principles and practices to the events and situations they encounter, unless they have a well-informed view of all the ramifications of inter-relationships, previously secured the solid support of a majority of leading politicians and have established the rules of engagement. As with most things in life, one's ability to deal with situations with which one is confronted varies directly with the amount of preparation and planning one has invested prior to the event.

Philosophy, principles and objectives are essentially matters for elected politicians but it is the responsibility of Chief Officers to ensure that the politicians successfully address the task of providing these essential prerequisites for the sound management of resources. The manager's job is to formulate and agree with Elected Members' strategy, tactics and micro-techniques.

                        INTERFACE

POLITICIANS   OFFICERS

PHILOSOPHY   ← - - - - →   MICRO-TECHNIQUES
    ↓   ↑
PRINCIPLES   ← - - - - →   TACTICS
    ↓   ↑
OBJECTIVES   ← - - - - →   STRATEGY

POLITICAL   CONTACT   MANAGERIAL
←──────   ──────→
DIRECTION   COMMUNICATION   INTERPRETATION

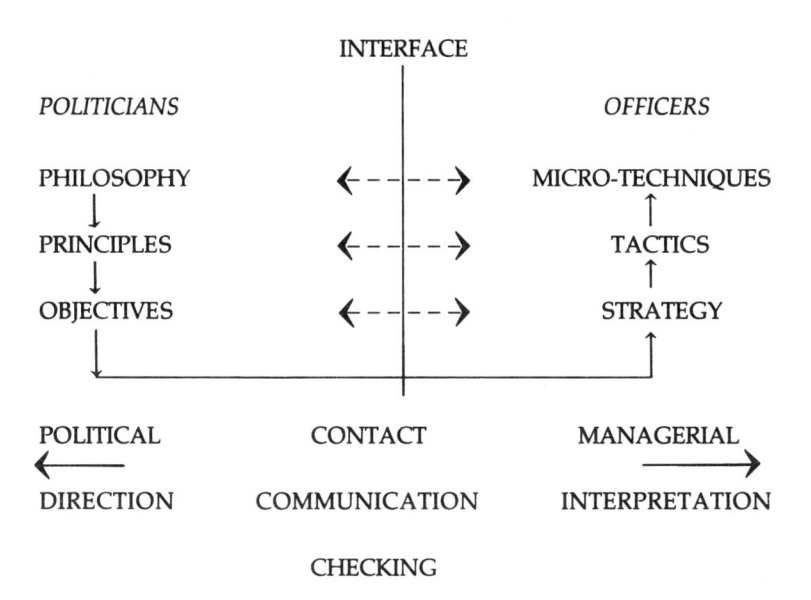

                       CHECKING

Fig. 14.2 Political relationships

Strategy represents the long-term view, maybe a five-year approach; tactics are essentially those arrangements which are applied in any 12-month period, and micro-techniques are the day-to-day practices by which inputs are converted into outputs and outputs make an impact on the service, demand or need which is to be met.

Mechanisms must be established by the manager to check that strategy is successfully meeting objectives, and here monitoring of the policy variable is essential on a regular basis. Communication and contract arrangements are essential to ensure that tactics are consistent with principles and that micro-techniques – the methods, practices and procedures with which staff engage the public – are consistent with the philosophy of the political administration.

The aim should be to create a healthy organization. Health is seldom attainable if hygiene is not attended to. The manager will be aware of the concept of 'hygiene factors', the presence of which will not ensure that an organization performs well, but the absence of which would certainly prevent the potential of the organization being fully attained. Essentially these hygiene factors are pay, conditions, the quality of the working environment, managerial consistency and employee confidence about equal opportunities including methods of selection and promotion.

The attainment of a healthy organization goes well beyond simply recognizing and dealing with these issues, however. If the organization's health is considered in terms of attaining a complete state of social, structural, philosophical, functional and economic well-being, then the primary consideration should be the recruitment, selection, training, deployment and management of human resources. The primary task is to secure a 'fit' between the organizational-development plan and the staff-development plan.

The staff-development plan must take on board the agenda of all employees, individually and collectively. Efficient and reliable contact and communication are central to the construction of a staff-development plan. Analysis of staff needs should be undertaken in such a way that it provides adequate data in three key areas: personal/career development, systems development and organizational development. Only proactive managers who invest time, energy and effort in human-resources planning and management can hope to cope with the pressures and demands of a highly charged and rapidly changing workplace environment within the cultural heritage which currently characterizes local government.

The tendency for local authorities as with other organizations will be to have flattened hierarchies, a reduced but highly skilled and highly paid core of Senior Officers, service-delivery peripherals with dedicated front-line staff operating on a very flexible basis when the public needs them, and access to fluctuating casual contract labour. It is better to plan for these changes and pursue them in collaboration with staff and trade unions rather than to be confronted by financial crises and commercial competition and be driven into rapid and traumatic change for which neither politicians nor trade unions have been psychologically prepared.

The traditional local authority management mould has been broken; so have many local authority senior managers. The future survival and success of local government will depend upon the resilience of those who remain and on their ability to apply the requisite skills to the new situation. Effective human-resources management is now at a premium and the survival of municipal enterprise depends upon the speed and scope of its application.

Part Three
Implications for managers: information sources

Rosemary Raddon

Introduction to Part Three

The last part of the book considers the management implications of the changes which are affecting people at work. These changes are considered in the widest sense, to include the political and economic world, as well as the changes in the composition and expectations of the workforce. Managers need to understand both the presented and hidden issues, and to be able to work with them. To do this they will not only have to be given support and training for themselves, but to offer this to their employees. In addition they will need access to information in a range of formats, as well as access to information from other managers through networking and informal contacts. Relevant supporting information obtainable from many sources, is also given in this part of the book.

15 Implications for managers

15.1 Coping with change

The management implications of these developments are many and varied. They embrace a range of issues, including philosophies, style, personal ideologies, organizational culture and values, psychodynamic concepts, economic and political factors, legislation and changing beliefs. The contexts are equally wide and as well as library and information services embrace education, training, research and consultancy, plus the whole gamut of personnel management and legislative practices. These in turn will have been determined largely by external pressures, such as social, political and economic changes. Management practices must also be seen in the context of theoretical developments. These range from the work of Etzioni,[1] concerned with the 'typology' of organizations, and the organizational theories of Handy.[2] Strategies developed by McGregor,[3] Mayo[4] and Likert[5] are part of this background, leading into the work of Herzberg[6] and Maslow[7] on job satisfaction. In the last few years there has been an enormous literature on the subject, reflecting the importance of good practice.

As a result the training, education and continuing education of managers is becoming increasingly important. Initiatives such as the Management Charter Initiative[8] code of practice, and the setting up of a national forum for management education and development are examples of new ideas. They build on theories of participative management, management by objectives, innovative, strategic and entrepreneurial management. CPD is assuming increasing importance. Total quality management is another current descriptor.

At present there are many forces which are causing turbulence and change for managers, particularly in the public sector. These can be identified as specifics within the broad parameters but are constantly shifting. Turbulence is also generated by large-scale organizations taking over and engulfing smaller practices, as part of global changes. Small may be beautiful, but the small can be lost within larger conglomerates, and so the feeling of 'holding' and care tends to be relinquished, provoking feelings of unease in workers. Such feelings of unease are reflections of childhood patterns of behaviour, which re-appear at times of stress. Changes in the importance and roles of skilled and craft workers, the decline in traditional industries, combined with growth in the newer technological industries, also produce tensions. Workers often reflect these fears, including those of being de-skilled, through industrial action, and managers have to try and resolve the conflicts. Such conflicts are often presentations of other, undefined problems, with individual concerns at the centre. Rapid organizational change, particularly in relatively structured organizations and in local authorities and education, can produce responses to change which are frequently negative. They arise out of the need for workers to defend what they perceive as attacks on themselves and their 'territory'. The feeling of being attacked is basic, and so produces child-like reactions, as workers respond through anger and destructive practices. Organizations and managers respond in a variety of ways, but the relationships between individuals and groups or layers, encompassing technological developments, social groupings, administrative structures, production areas and policy areas, will respond, group and re-group, depending on the apparent pressures.

Managers and personnel managers, particularly, may be in a position in which it is difficult to implement concern for the individual, especially those in large organizations where individuals have to be seen to be cost-effective. The non-earning manager or employee is seen to be a secondary force in many organizations. These changes indicate a need for union support and understanding, to ensure that developments do not work against the individual. It is also needed to ensure that too much turbulence in the workplace is avoided, leading to decreased involvement in the product, be it information services or tins of baked beans. Too much confusion will lead to increased and non-productive involvement in conflict activities.

Size, culture, tradition and objectives, all vary from organization to organization and contribute to tensions. Managers are part of this culture and need to understand their roles within it. Roles can relate to interaction between individuals and between groups, and will reflect these cultures and values. Shared values can contribute to the work of groups, or can get lost if groups and individuals are confused or uncertain about their relationships with other groups and individuals. Defences will then be formed by threatening and anti management behaviour. Individuals and groups can hold the anger for an organization, and this can be seen in many industrial-action patterns of behaviour.

In this current context of rapid change, management can act as the focus for 'bad' feelings, whereby individuals split and project their own feelings onto management as a defence mechanism. This can be illustrated by direct confrontation, such as industrial action, or indirect confrontation, illustrated by behaviour at meetings or between groups. Managers may find it helpful to understand some of the dynamics of these situations, both in the way in which they relate to their own individual unconscious drives, and to the way in which these drives are reflected in group reactions. Education and training in these areas is important. The tensions between group tasks and group loyalties are also relevant. The reasons for and effects of some management styles also need to be understood and, equally important, the fundamental reasons for the behaviour. In turn the response of the worker cannot be understood without some knowledge of what activated that response.

The effective manager needs also to be aware of the overt and covert behaviour in the organization. Overt behaviour is relatively easy to relate to pressures and tensions, but covert behaviour is part of the hidden and often unconscious behaviour of individuals. Some understanding of self, as well as the theories of personal development, linked for example to the work of Klein[9] and Winnicott,[10] are an added strength. They underpin the manager who really wants to understand the needs and motives of individuals and the organization. Organizational and personal development and understanding are no longer a luxury, but essential.

The individual, the group, the organization and the culture are crucial elements for the good manager to understand and work with. Action learning, counselling and coaching skills, all supplement traditional managerial skills and are increasingly being made available. They enhance with and support negotiating skills, as well as other personal relationships.

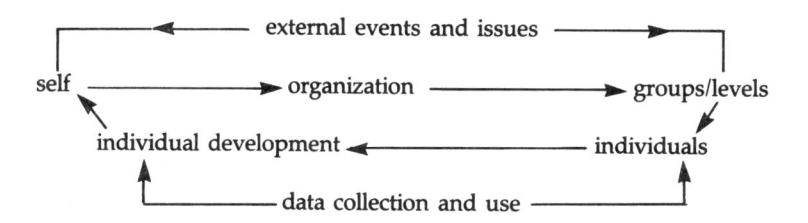

Fig. 15.1 Management circles

A structure which understands the feelings of the powerless, as well as of the powerful, can begin to understand some of the issues which workers need to resolve, if they are to be integrated into the organization and be at ease with themselves. Those perceived to have power, the managers, are also perceived as the enemy and so are the victims of the organizational unease. But if managers understand the dynamics of this projection, it can be seen as part of the total dynamic. Language, roles, relationships and boundaries are also important aspects of an understanding of the self. As indicated, managers need to understand themselves, in relation to why they react in certain ways in certain situations. What happens to their feelings when ideologies and confusions are split off from groups and individuals and projected onto them? What happens when they are unable to 'control' situations? Such questions are all part of the process of change. There is a need to understand the motivation behind career and organizational moves, in personal and developmental terms. This is an area of specific relevance to women, who may feel they have been under-achievers, as a result of sibling or peer pressure, or from following social norms. Alternatively, ambition which is perceived as having been achieved may produce guilt that those peers or siblings may be hurt in the process of achievement, so ambitions may again be buried. Frequently strong defences are built up against the guilt this behaviour produces, with more and more behavioural patterns reinforcing the guilt. A denial of the female aspect of the manager can be very destructive. Such conflicts are often unconsciously avoided, but may be manifested in union activities or disruptive work patterns. Reasons for achievement are equally important to understand.

More people feel vulnerable if their weaknesses are perceived and so defence mechanisms hide insecurities which can often be traced back to childhood behaviour and circumstances. Such behavioural patterns are then replayed in adult life, but can be detrimental to personal relations, especially in industrial relations. Both sides replay such activities and neither attempts to cross the barricades. Communication becomes confused and difficult.

Personal relationships are part of the learning process, with transactions taking place between groups and individuals, all bringing their own personal and unique experiences to the situation. These form the basis of an understanding of the workforce and help to defuse potential confrontational issues in industrial relations.

Managers need an understanding of these areas, as well as inherent personal qualities, including intuition, leadership qualities, empathy, control, decision-making abilities, analytical skills and flexible attitudes. They should also acquire skills through training, continuing education and self-development. These skills should include counselling, communications skills, organizational theories, group theories, psychodynamic theories, planning skills and target setting, delegation skills, and education and training theories. A possible 'match' between individuals and their own aspirations, as well as organizational aspirations, is the ultimate goal.

References
1. Etzioni, A., *A comparative analysis of complex organisations*, 2nd ed., New York, Free Press, 1975.
2. Handy, C., *The making of managers*, London, MSC/NEDO/BIMI, 1987.
3. McGregor, D., *The human side of enterprise*, New York, McGraw-Hill, 1960.
4. Mayo, E., *Human problems of an industrial civilisation*, Boston, Harvard Business School, 1946.
5. Likert, R., *The human organization*, New York, McGraw-Hill, 1967.
6. Herzberg, F., *The motivation to work*, 2nd ed., London, Chapman and Hall, 1959.
7. Maslow, A. H., *Motivation and personality*, London, Harper and Row, 1970.
8. Management Charter Initiative, *Proposed national framework for management development*, London, CMED, 1988.
9. Klein, M., *Our adult world and its roots in infancy*, London, Heinemann, 1963.
10. Winnicott, D. W., *The family and individual development*, London, Tavistock, 1965.

Further reading
Buchanan, D. A. and Huczynski, A. A., *Organizational behaviour*, London, Prentice Hall, 1985.
De Board, R., *The psychoanalysis of organisations*, London, Tavistock, 1978.
Jones, K., *Conflict and change in library organisations*, London, Bingley, 1984.
Marris, P., *Loss and change*, London, Routledge and Kegan Paul, 1974.
Training Commission, *Classifying the components of management competences*, London, Training Commission, 1988.

Manager's notes

Understand change and its political, psychological and social bases
Understand the culture of the organization
Try to understand individual and group behaviour
Relate this to an understanding of self
Develop good management practices
Support these at all levels in appropriate ways
Support change

15.2 The political aspects of change

Background
This section is an attempt to provide an overview and brief analysis of some of the major factors influencing the political process and, by inference, the managers involved in this process of change. The wider issues of democracy, accountability, social philosophies, and ideological power bases are dealt with in the literature, and are considered here in relation to their general influence on issues. Within this broad context, elected Members are also involved in confusing messages, and are caught up between the Scylla of purist politics, of either complexion, and the Charybdis of vote-winning service delivery. Those involved in the management process are inevitably also caught up in these currents, and traditional models of operation do not necessarily provide the most effective support. However, it is possible to identify some of the factors which at the moment are contributing to the process of change. The main factors to be considered and analysed are, of course, the political forces of right, left or centre, or a combination of all three, as these determine the parameters of service, and what emphases are placed where. Difficulties arise when these forces change direction, backtrack, or form different coalitions. Services which have then been directed onto one path have to be directed onto another, difficult for most staff and difficult in resources terms – frequently policy changes are expensive in financial and human resources. For example, a policy shift away from race relations and women's units, not seen as popular with many voters, is an illustration of resource allocation shifting in response to political ideas. The pattern varies in relation to political ideologies.

Decentralization and devolution as alternatives to existing bureaucracies can also be seen as an example of political change – in a move away from the traditional paternalistic/maternalistic 'we know best' approach, to a community-centred or service-based model of delivery. This involves changes in the traditional models of political power, professionalism, and the necessary bureaucracy to implement policies. Tensions between centrist control and local small units of control or service delivery are also part of the debate. The concepts of 'professionalism' are also in a state of flux, as each profession tries to match needs, and professional education, within constantly shifting pressures. Such changes immediately produce changes in power and authority lines, and a constant shift in focus – what and where is the centre, and who makes the final policy decisions? What is then the role of the local elected councillor? Other questions arise, such as could and should not consumers have a say in and choice of the services provided for and by them? Such a pluralistic move to make the party, the machinery, and the services accessible, still produces confusions and cross-currents, even though it is an essential element in linking left-wing ideology and grass roots thinking and feeling. The balance between services, innovation, the injection of new ideas, management strategies, and users has to be maintained, and quality of access cannot be diluted during the debate. Issues relating to the system and accountability arise – do the so-called professionals make decisions, or the consumers, and if so, using what criteria, and how can these relationships be established and some kind of working balance be achieved? What are the factors that really affect decision making and resource allocation? (The vociferous pressure groups, all with differing power bases, and their demands are now a familiar part of local political life). Yet it has to be admitted that in some cases the resources and services provided by the professionals do not provide an answer or a relevant service to the consumer. The right wing is also offering choice in theory, through consumer forces and the process of market forces.

Policy conflicts are also reflected in requests for resources, assuming that there is a finite limit on spending – should services to the housebound old take precedence over provision for the under fives, or the Asian elderly, the information services, or other groups who are frequently excluded from service delivery for one reason or another? All may be politically acceptable, some or all may have their roots in community politics, and how can they be prioritized in relation to reference services, schools services, etc.? Many librarians would argue that this is 'professional' judgement, but this view is seen by many left wingers as obstructing the cause of local decision-making and involvement. This in turn links with the 'anti officer' syndrome, causing yet more turbulence.

The Catch 22 situation then consists of a service which doesn't appear to have the same priorities as the elected members, and so fails to attract resources, or does happen to have the flavour-of-the-month, but loses resources when that flavour is swept away, recycled, or loses credibility for a range of reasons.

Policy conflicts also exist in a covert way, seen in some of the personal alliances which have been formed and destroyed. They may add to the flavour-of-the-month syndrome, and achieve resources in the short term, but are dangerous alliances to pursue. Also, the 'complicity of interest' and relationships between members and union officials at ward level adds to the complex situation, but can be a valuable way of getting more political fingers into the resource pie.

'Internal' political processes are not necessarily reflective of the external ones. In theory, as mentioned before, services and processes reflect those external policies and decisions, but that isn't always, and can't always, be so. All the theorizing about participation and communication obscures the fact that officers have, and probably always will have, their own views and ideologies, and even though they may in public toe the party line, can in fact be quite subversive behind the scenes, and add to tensions.

Many Members are inexperienced (politically) but have strong ideological views, and so disregard officers' perceptions of service priorities, which have frequently been obtained as a result of many years in the field. As a result of political decisions, the user/consumer may then receive a lower standard of service delivery than officers may think is acceptable. Environmental health, records management and building operations are all examples of areas where there are potential and actual ideological conflicts. A lack of political consensus makes concentrated policy development very difficult, and ideological clashes can weaken programmes. At a practical level many committees represent, on either side of the spectrum, a wide range of beliefs, and officers have to operate in relation to the apparent power bases. These also shift, and so again changes can be swift and in some cases counter-productive in terms of services.

Also the union situation is very volatile at the moment, without a common aim of improved service delivery from both management and the unions. Some 'hard' left wing elements are currently infiltrating NALGO, bringing the class war into the negotiating arena, and so the concept of 'service' gets lost. This concept of service is part of the shared values idea, which is so important. Many of the new ideas are directly and inherently anti-management, for some of the reasons mentioned earlier, and as a result in many cases the unions are in direct opposition to their employing authorities.

A recent quote from NALGO in an unnamed London Borough to a new employee – 'we are anti-management here' (genuine quote!) is another example. The constant conflict between union and management erodes initiatives and deflates and negates services. It also illustrates unconscious processes at work. The paradox of this situation is that if managers succeed in one service area, then others are castigated for not achieving a similar standard, or are toppled from their position of 'excellence', as Members do not welcome criticism from those areas where services are not efficient and particularly if they are in their home wards. This contributes to a limited life span of officers, which, combined with the political lack of experience, increases management instability and staff turnover, with an almost inevitable decline in services. The recent number of appointments at Director level indicates the increasing speed of staff turnover, with all the ensuing instability that this causes. So-called 'crisis management' is merely a reflection of some of this turmoil. Women and members of disadvantaged groups can sometimes be used as pawns in this process – appointed within an equal opportunities policy, but not supported as managers, or allowed to manage the internal prioritization process. Although not explicitly stated, there also has not been wholehearted support by all unions for equal-opportunity policies, and this encourages potential ideological and racial conflict between party and union, and supports institutionalized racism. Token collusion by several forces weakens still further the real development of services to those who are normally excluded to a large extent, and so negates the ideological rhetoric.

Conflict tension between caring/sharing open democratic management, involving staff in the management of the organization and in personal assessment, counselling and advice, is seen as yet another example of perfidious management seeking to gain (capitalist) power at the expense of the workers, and is an example of the classic left-wing theoretical struggle, yet may happen where both sides may in fact be on the same side, and indeed often are, of the ideological line or of the barricades.

In theory the users and the workers should be supporting each other, but in practice this is not so. Many union practices are very restrictive, so providing the opportunity for fewer changes and less sensitivity to community needs. But any failure in service is inevitably blamed on management, and the circle is perpetuated, fuelled by current government thinking, creating some of the turbulence mentioned earlier.

The confused lines over the proliferation of community groups do not help clarify the process of management, and lead to conflicts over resources, and their control between the statutory and voluntary sectors. Groups who previously moved 'inside' and 'outside' of the party machinery, now sometimes move together, causing more blurred lines. Also, as Melissa Benn[1] said in a recent article on feminism, some people get caught up in the delights of manipulating the party machinery, while forgetting the 'cause' that made them take on the machinery in the first place. The corollary of this, as already reflected in some of the union situations, is the infiltration of any party machinery from hard left and hard right, so creating still further splits and coalitions, which add to an uneven and unsettled situation. A similar confusion arises when people are appointed at a senior level because of their political affiliations (as happens equally in right- and left-wing organizations), then cannot improve service delivery, are encouraged to leave, and so a vacuum is left, probably filled by another figurehead, with even less experience and professional expertise, and so the spiral descends downwards once more. This works against innovation and the maintenance of the status quo. At the same time high standards of service are frequently expected, but cannot be delivered for this range of reasons. The paradox here is between the high demand on one hand, and the default factor on the other. In many right-wing authorities service delivery is of a very high standard, but is obtained at the expense of workers' rights. In some left-wing authorities the appointment of officers for their anti-council views (or perhaps anti-bureaucratic and anti- 'the system' views), takes place as part of a radical attack on an authority by members who want to see change, and who view many officers as obstacles in the way of achieving the revolution. This syndrome can and does add to the confusion, and instead of forging alliances between officers, creates further rifts. Managing the political process also includes equal-opportunities and race policies, stemming from internal and external forces. The pitfalls of tokenism, and the need to deal with issues which are seen as threats by the male-dominated unions, are also areas of conflict which can be identified.

Within this current context, the focus on the manager becomes important both in terms of survival, and in terms of change. Questions arise which in turn require more change, which in turn requires some kind of professional, personal, social or political bedrock on which to base those changes.

Currently emerging in the management arena is the perception of a 'feminine style' of management, which is *not* about being nice to people and listening to everyone's problems, but an ethos which is different from the traditional male dominated top-down model. To quote Richardson out of context – 'women want a different cake, not just a bigger share of the same cake'. This concept relates to training, as it is concerned not only with personal development, but with the rejection of a training model that is concerned with the 'deficiencies' of women managers. It seeks to establish a range of different parameters.

The paradox of 'feminine management' is that on one hand it forms an ideal objective for many women who have rejected the male model, and do not want to be male clones, but at the same time allows the system, and particularly the male dominated unions, to corrupt both the person and the system, so that there is a dilemma – should one try and change the system, but at great cost and possibly failure, or connive at the situation which exists but which is personally rejected? This is another complex area which needs

more investigation as part of the changing political scene.
Shared values also relate to the McKinsey framework for organizations referred to in Peters and Waterman.[2] This is another factor in the debate on managing the political process. This concept of overall style or shared values is apparently easier to foster or focus on in the private than in the public sector, but this 'core' of the process is also the core of some of our dilemmas. In the force field analysis comparison, (the area in the centre, the middle of the sandwich), should be the area for growth and development, but instead seems to be in a continuous state of turmoil. In management terms this whole process is thus a series of contradictions and difficulties which are hard to reconcile, to share, or to disseminate.

As a final comment: 'one should stress the significance which, in the modern world, political parties have in the elaboration and diffusion of conceptions of the world, because essentially what they do is to work out the ethics and the politics corresponding to these conceptions and act as it were as their historical "laboratory"' (Gramsci, 1987).[3]

References
1 Benn, M., 'Sisters and slogans', *Marxism today*, April 1987, 26–8.
2 Peters, T. J. and Waterman, R. H., *In search of excellence*, New York, Harper & Row, 1982.
3 Gramsci, A., *Selections from political writings*, London, Lawrence and Wishart, 1987.

Further reading
Blondell, J. and Hall, R., 'Conflict, decision making and the perceptions of local councillors', *Political studies* 15, 1967, 338–48.
Gramsci, A., *Letters from prison*, London, Cape, 1975.
Gyford, J., 'The new urban left: a local road to socialism?', *New society*, 21 April 1983, 91–3.
Gyford, J., 'Our changing councillor', *New society*, 3 May 1984, 181–3.
Hambleton, R. and Hoggett, P. (eds.), *The politics of decentralisation*, Bristol, School for Advanced Urban Studies, 1984.
Jones, K., *Conflict and change in library organisations*, London, Bingley, 1984.
Line, M., 'Requirements for library and information work and the role of library education', *Education for information*, 1, 1983, 25–37.
Local Government Reform: short version of the report of the Royal Commission on Local Government in England, London, HMSO, 1989, Cmnd 4039 (Maud Report).

Local Government Training Board, *Decentralised resource management: an issue paper*, Luton, Local Government Training Board, 1986.

McKinsey & Co Inc., 55 East 22nd Street, New York, New York 10022.

National Consumer Council, *Measuring up: consumer assessment of local authority services*, London, National Consumer Council, 1986.

Peat Marwick, McLintock, *Current issues in public sector management*, London, Peat Marwick, 1986.

Report of the Committee of Inquiry into the local authority services. London, HMSO, 1986, Cmnd 1797 (Widdicombe Report).

Shavitt, D., *The politics of public librarianship*, New York, Greenwood Press, 1986.

Stewart, J., *Local government: the conditions of local choice*, London, Allen & Unwin for Institute of Local Government Studies, 1983.

Stewart, J., 'Bureaucracy and decentralisation in the delivery of local authority services', in Hambleton, R. and Hoggett, P. (eds.), *The politics of decentralisation*, Bristol, School for Advanced Urban Studies, 1984.

UGC/NAB, *Report of the Transbinary Group on Librarianship and Information Studies*, London, UGC/NAB, 1986.

Usherwood, B., 'The elected member and the public library', *Public library journal*, **2** (5), Sept/Oct 1987, 71–5.

Women in libraries newsletter, No. 34, November/December 1986 (Complete issue).

Wintou, P., 'Local councils: breaking the chains', *New statesman*, **14**, January 1983, 8–10.

Yorke, D. A. (ed.), 'The marketing of local authority leisure services', *European journal of marketing*, **18** (2), 1984 (Complete issue).

Manager's notes

Understand the dynamics of political change
Relate these to organizational change
Relate these to changes in service delivery
Support staff who have to effect these changes
Be involved in the processes as well as the planning
Watch the hidden agendas
Manage the political process

16 Abbreviations and glossary

ACAS	Advisory, Conciliation and Arbitration Service
ACTS	White-collar branch of Transport and General Workers' Union
ACTT	Association of Cinematograph, Television and Allied Technicians
AEUW	Amalgamated Union of Engineering Workers
ALA	Associate of the Library Association
ALCL	Association of London Chief Librarians
AMA	Association of Metropolitan Authorities
AMMA	Associate Masters' and Mistresses' Association
APEX	Association of Professional, Executive, Clerical and Computer Staff
APT	Association of Polytechnic Teachers
APT&C	Administrative, Professional, Technical and Clerical grades (of workers)
ASLIB	Association for Information Management
ASTMS	Association of Scientific, Technical and Managerial Staff (now MSS)
AUEW	Amalgamated Union of Engineering Workers
AUT	Association of University Teachers
BETA	Broadcasting and Entertainments Trades Alliance
Bridlington	TUC agreement and guidelines for regulating the way in which unions recruit members
CBI	Confederation of British Industry
CCT	Competitive Contract Tendering
CICI	Confederation of Information and Communications Industries
CIPFA	Chartered Institute of Public Finance and Accountancy
CLEA	Council for Local Education Authorities
COHSE	Confederation of Health Service Employees
COPOL	Committee of Polytechnic Librarians
CPD	Continuing Professional Development
CPSA	Civil and Public Services Association
CRE	Commission for Racial Equality
CSU	Civil Services Union
CVCP	Committee of Vice-Chancellors and Principals
DES	Department of Education and Science
EEPTU	Electrical, Engineering and Plumbing Trades Union
EOC	Equal Opportunities Commission

ERA	Education Reform Act
FE	Further Education
FEU	Further Education Unit
FOLACL	Federation of Local Authority Chief Librarians
FUMPO	Federated Union of Managers and Professional Officers
GLC	Greater London Council
GLES	Greater London Employers Secretariat
GMB	General Municipal Boilermakers
HEC	Higher Education Corporation
IIS	Institute of Information Scientists
ILEA	Inner London Education Authority
IPCS	Institute of Professional Civil Servants
IPM	Institute of Personnel Management
IPMS	Institute of Professionals, Managers and Specialists
IRSF	Inland Revenue Staff Association
LA	Library Association
LACSAB	Local Authority Conditions of Service Advisory Board (now Local Government Management Board)
LAMSAC	Local Authorities Management Services and Computer Committee (now Local Government Management Board)
LEA	Local Education Authority
LGMB	Local Government Management Board
LGTB	Local Government Training Board
LIP	Library and Information Plan
LMS	Local Management of Schools
MATSA	Managerial, Administration, Technical and Supervisory Association
MCI	Management Charter Initiative
MSC	Manpower Services Commission
MSS	Manufacturing, Science and Finance
NAB	National Advisory Body
NALGO	National and Local Government Officers' Association
NAS/UWT	National Association of Schoolmasters and the Union of Women Teachers
NATFHE	National Association of Teachers in Further and Higher Education
NCVQ	National Council for Vocational Qualifications
NGA	National Graphical Association

NJC	National Joint Council for Local Authorities Services, Administrative, Professional, Technical and Clerical Staff/Manual Workers
NUJ	National Union of Journalists
NUM	National Union of Mineworkers
NUPE	National Union of Public Employees
NUR	National Union of Railwaymen
NUT	National Union of Teachers
OAL	Office of Arts and Libraries
PAT	Professional Association of Teachers
PCFC	Polytechnics and Colleges Funding Council
PCNNC	Polytechnics and Colleges National Negotiating Committee
SCL	Society of County Librarians
SMCCL	Society of Municipal and County Chief Librarians
SOGAT	Society of Graphical and Allied Trades
SRB	Special Review Body, set up by the TUC to cover services to members, recruitment and negotiations over single-union agreements
TA	Training Agency (now Training Enterprise and Education Directorate)
TASS(AUEW)	Technical, Administrative and Supervisory Section (of Amalgamated Union of Engineering Workers)
TEC	Training and Enterprise Council
TEED	Training Enterprise and Education Directorate
TGWU	Transport and General Workers' Union
TSSA	Transport Salaried Staff Association
TUC	Trades Union Congress
UCATT	Union of Construction, Allied Trades and Technicians
UCW	Union of Communication Workers
UDM	Union of Democratic Mineworkers
UFC	Universities Funding Council
UGC	University Grants Committee
USDAW	Union of Shop Distributive and Allied Workers

17 Bibliography

ACAS (Advisory, Conciliation and Arbitration Service), *Absence*, London, ACAS, 1983 (Advisory booklet No. 5).
ACAS, *The ACAS role in conciliation, arbitration and mediation*, London, ACAS, 1982.
ACAS, *Annual report 1988*, London, ACAS, 1989.
ACAS, *Annual report 1989*, London, ACAS, 1990.
ACAS, *Collective bargaining in Britain: its extent and level*, London, ACAS, 1983 (Discussion paper No. 2).
ACAS, *Conciliation, arbitration, mediation in trade disputes*, London, ACAS, 1983.
ACAS, *Conciliation between individuals and employers*, London, ACAS, 1987.
ACAS, *Developments in harmonisation*, London, ACAS, 1982 (Discussion paper No. 1).
ACAS, *Disciplinary practice and procedures in employment*, London, HMSO, 1977 (Code of practice 1).
ACAS, *Discipline at work: the ACAS advisory handbook*, London, ACAS, 1987.
ACAS, *Employment handbook*, London, ACAS, 1990.
ACAS, *Employing people: the ACAS handbook for small firms*, London, ACAS, 1985.
ACAS, *Employment policies*, New ed., London, ACAS, 1986 (Advisory booklet No. 10).
ACAS, *Improving industrial relations: a joint responsibility*, New ed., London, ACAS, 1986.
ACAS, *Individual employment rights: ACAS conciliation between individuals and employers*, New ed., London, ACAS, 1987.
ACAS, *An industrial relations handbook*, London, ACAS, 1980.
ACAS, *Meeting the challenge of change: case studies [from the] Department of Employment Work Research Unit*, London, Work Research Unit, Department of Employment, 1982.
ACAS, *Redundancy arrangements: the 1986 ACAS survey*, London, ACAS, 1987 (Occasional paper 37).
ACAS, *Time off for trade union duties and activities*, London, HMSO, 1977 (Code of practice 3).
ACAS, *Using ACAS in industrial disputes*, London, ACAS, 1987.
Allen, R., *How to prepare a case for an industrial tribunal*, 2nd ed., Manchester, EOC, 1987.
Analysing industrial relations, Sheffield, MSC, 1978.
Anthony, P. D., *Conduct of industrial relations*, London, IPM, 1977.

Apslund, G., *Women managers: changing organisational cultures*, London, Wiley, 1988.
Armstrong, M., *Handbook of personnel management practice*, London, Kogan Page, 1988.
Ascher, K., *The politics of privatisation*, London, Macmillan, 1987.
Ashridge Management College/MSC, *No barriers here?: a guide to career development issues in the employment of women*, London, Sheffield, MSC, 1981.
Attwood, M., *Developing equal opportunities at work*, Cambridge, Employment Relations, 1986.
Audit Commission, *Competitiveness and on trading out of local authorities services*, London, Audit Commission, 1987 (Occasional paper No. 3).
Audit Commission, *Economy, efficiency and effectiveness*, London, Audit Commission, 1984.
Audit Commission, *Improving economy, efficiency, and effectiveness in the public sector*, London, Audit Commission, 1983.
Audit Commission, *Performance review in local government: a handbook for auditors and local authorities*, London, HMSO, 1986.
Backhouse, R., 'Library services trade unions – ignored or forgotten?', *Assistant librarian*, 1977, 82–5.
Backhouse, R., *Information services for trade unionists*, London, British Library, 1982 (BL research and development report 5695).
Backhouse, R., 'Striking lessons', *Library Association record*, **86** (8), 1984, 294.
Bain, G. S., *The growth of white collar unionisation*, London, Oxford University Press, 1970.
Bain, G. S. and Price, R., *Profiles of union growth: a comparative statistical portrait of eight countries*, Oxford, Blackwell, 1980.
Bain, G. S. and Woolven, G. B., *Bibliography of British industrial relations*, London, Oxford University Press, 1979.
Balmforth, C., 'New technology and the trade unions', *UCR newsletter*, **8**, 1982, 3–12.
Bamber, G., *Militant managers?: managerial unionism and industrial relations*, Aldershot, Gower, 1986.
Bassett, P., 'All together now?', *Marxism today*, Jan 1989, 44–7.
Bayliss, D., *The Barchester Engineering case – a training exercise on industrial tribunals*, Sheffield, Sheffield Polytechnic, PAVIC Publications, 1986.
Beloff, M., *Sex discrimination: the new law*, London, Butterworth, 1976.
Beresford, P. and Grice, A., 'Another giant union to defy the TUC', *Sunday times*, 14 August 1988, no. 8558, 1 and 2.
Biblarz, D. and others, 'Professional associates and unions: future

impact of today's decisions', *College and research libraries*, **36**, 1975, 121-8.

Bichteler, J., 'Technostress in libraries: causes, effects and solutions', *Electronic library*, **5**, 1987, 282-7.

Biddle, D., *Human aspects of management*, London, IPM, 1980.

Bion, W. R., *Experiences in groups*, London, Tavistock, 1961.

Bion, W. R., *Learning from experiences*, London, Heinemann, 1962.

Blackburn, R., *Union character and social class*, London, Batsford, 1967.

Blunkett, D. and Jackson, K., *Democracy in crisis: the Town Halls respond*, London, Hogarth Press, 1987.

Boot, R. L., Cowling, A. G. and Stanworth, M. J. K., *Behavioural sciences for managers*, London, Edward Arnold, 1982.

Bowers, J., *A practical approach to employment law*, London, Financial Training Publications, 1982.

Bowers, J. and Duggan, M., *The modern law of strikes*, London, Croner Publications, 1988.

Boydell, T. and Pedler, M. (eds.), *Management self-development*, Aldershot, Gower, 1981.

Braham, P., Rhodes, E. and Pearn, M. (eds.), *Discrimination and disadvantage in employment*, London, Haver and Ren, 1981.

Brown, C., *Black and white Britain*, London, Policy Studies Institute, 1984.

Brown, R., *Group processes*, Oxford, Blackwell, 1988.

Buchanan, D. A. and Huczynski, A. A., *Organizational behaviour*, London, Prentice Hall, 1985.

Burns, T. and Stalker, G. M., *The management of innovation*, London, Tavistock, 1961.

Burrington, G., *Equal opportunities in librarianship? gender and career aspirations*, London, Library Association Publishing, 1987.

Burrows, G., *'No strike' agreements and pendulum arbitration*, London, IPM, 1986.

Butcher, H. et al, *Local government and Thatcherism*, London, Routledge, 1989.

Byrne, T., *Local government in Britain*, 3rd ed., London, Penguin, 1985.

Carby, K. and Thakur, M., *No problems here?*, London, IPM, 1977.

Carpenter, S. L. and Kennedy, W. J. D., *Managing public disputes: a practical guide to handling conflict and reaching agreement*, London, Jossey-Bass, 1988.

Case studies in industrial relations training, Cambridge, Employment Relations, Sheffield, MSC, 1987.

Casey, D., 'The emerging role of set advisor in action learning programmes', *Journal of European training*, **5** (3), 1976, 3-4.

Canyon, W., 'Collective bargaining and professional development of academic librarians', *College and research libraries*, **43**, 1982, 132-9.
Central Arbitration Committee, *Annual report 1988*, London, CAC, 1989.
Centre for Professional Employment Counselling, *Tenth anniversary essay competition*, Bromley, CEPEC, 1988 (Occasional papers No. 3).
Chartered Institute of Public Finance and Accountancy, *Performance indicators in schools*, London, CIPFA, 1988.
Coates, C., *Trade unions and industrial relations: a reader's guide*, London, Library Association, Public Libraries Group, 1979.
Collinson, D., *Barriers to fair selection*, London, HMSO, 1988.
Commission for Racial Equality (CRE), *Code of practice for the elimination of racial discrimination*, London, CRE, 1983.
CRE, *Equal opportunity, positive action and young people*, London, CRE, 1983.
CRE, *Guide to the Race Relations Act 1976: employment*, London, CRE, 1984.
CRE, *Implementing equal employment opportunity policies*, London, CRE, 1983.
CRE, *Monitoring an equal opportunity policy: guide for employers*, London, CRE, 1984.
CRE, *Positive action and equal opportunity in employment*, London, CRE, 1985.
CRE, *Review of the Race Relations Act 1976: proposals for change*, London, CRE, 1985.
CRE, *Why keep ethnic records?*, London, CRE, 1984.
Committee of Vice-Chancellors and Principals and University Grants Committee, *University management statistics and performance indicators*, London, CVCP, 1988.
Competitive tendering in the public sector – the personnel implications, London, IPM, 1986.
Confederation of British Industry (CBI), *The Trade Unions Act 1984*, London, CBI, 1984.
CBI, *Equal pay for work of equal value*, London, CBI, 1984.
CBI, *Being a better neighbour*, London, CBI, 1985.
CBI, *Managing change*, London, CBI, 1985.
CBI, *Management skills*, London, CBI, 1988.
CBI, *Training in negotiation*, London, CBI, 1988.
Coombe, G., 'Reviewing the situation: performance reviews in Surrey', *Public library journal*, **2** (5), 1987, 77-81.
Cooper, C. (ed.), *Practical approaches to women's career development*, London, MSC, 1982.

Cooper, L. J., 'A research guide to the law of private-sector labor-management relations', *Law library journal,* 79 (3), 1987, 387–418.

Cosmo, G. and Lewis, N., *The role of ACAS conciliation in equal pay and sex discrimination cases,* Manchester, Equal Opportunities Commission, 1985.

Counselling at work, Bromley, Centre for Professional Employment Counselling, 1987 (Occasional paper No. 1).

Coventry Workshop, *Coventry Workshop at the crossroads,* Coventry, Coventry Workshop, 1980.

Coyle, A., *Redundant women,* London, Women's Press, 1984.

Crawshaw, I. C., 'Fraught years ahead?', *Assistant librarian,* 77 (2), February 1984, 20–2.

Croner's employee benefits 1988, Kingston, Croner Publications, 1988.

Croner's employment law, Kingston, Croner Publications, 1980.

Croner's guide to absence, Kingston, Croner Publications,

Croner's guide to discipline, Kingston, Croner Publications,

Croner's guide to fair dismissal, Kingston, Croner Publications,

Croner's guide to health and safety at work, Kingston, Croner Publications, 1987.

Croner's guide to interviews, Kingston, Croner Publications,

Croner's personnel law and practice, Kingston, Croner Publications,

Croner's personnel procedures, Kingston, Croner Publications, 1987.

Croner's personnel records, Kingston, Croner Publications,

Croner's reference book for employers, Kingston, Croner Publications,

Croner's Employment Law Department, *Fresh start – a positive approach to redundancy,* Kingston, Croner Publications, 1986.

Cruzat, G. S., 'Collective bargaining and the library manager', *Journal of library administration,* 7 (4), 1986, 67–82.

Cunningham, M., *Non-wage benefits,* London, Pluto, 1981.

Cunningham, M., *Non-wage benefits: 'fringe' benefits: what they are and how to win them,* London, Pluto, 1981.

Customer care – the personnel implications, London, Incomes Data Services/Institute of Personnel Management, 1990.

Davis, J. H., *Group performance,* London, Addison-Wesley, 1969.

De Board, R., *Counselling people at work: an introductory guide for managers,* London, Gower, 1983.

De Board, R., *The psychoanalysis of organisations,* London, Tavistock, 1978.

Democracy in trade unions, London, HMSO, 1983.

Department of Employment, *Directory of employers' associations, trade unions and joint organisations, etc.,* London, Department of Employment, 1988.

Department of Employment, *Suspension on medical grounds under health and safety regulations*, London, Department of Employment, 1989.
Dickens, L., Townsend, B. and Winchester, D., *Tackling sex discrimination through collective bargaining*, Manchester, EOC, 1988.
Dove, J., 'Librarians and NALGO', *Library world*, 72, 1970, 73–85.
Drucker, H. et al. (eds.), *Developments in British politics*, London, Macmillan, 1984.
Drucker, P. F., *Innovations and entrepreneurship*, London, Heinemann, 1985.
Education Reform Act, London, HMSO, 1988.
Eggleston, J. and others, *Education for some*, Stoke-on-Trent, Trentham, 1986.
Ellis, V., *The role of trade unions in the promotion of equal opportunities*, Manchester, EOC and Social Science Research Council, 1981.
Employment Act 1988, London, HMSO, 1988.
'Employment Act 1988', *Employment digest*, **249**, 1988, 1–8.
Employment facts, Sheffield, MSC, 1983.
Employment for the 1990s, London, HMSO, 1988.
Employment Training, *Equal opportunities code of practice*, Sheffield, Training Commission, 1988.
'Equal opportunities 1988', *Library Association record*, **91** (1), 1989, 33–4.
Equal Opportunities Commission (EOC), *Annual report*, Manchester, EOC, 1988.
EOC, *Code of practice*, Manchester, EOC, 1985.
EOC, *Equal opportunities: a guide for employers*, rev. ed., Manchester, EOC, 1988.
EOC, *Equal treatment of men and women: strengthening the acts*, Manchester, EOC, 1987.
EOC, *Equality at work: a guide to the employment provisions of the Sex Discrimination Act 1975*, Manchester, EOC, 1982.
EOC, *Fair and effective selection: guidance on equal opportunities policies in recruitment and selection procedures*, Manchester, EOC, 1986.
EOC, *Guidelines for equal opportunities employers*, Manchester, EOC, 1986.
EOC, *Job evaluation schemes free of sex bias*, Manchester, EOC, 1956.
EOC, *Men's jobs? Women's jobs?*, Manchester, EOC, 1986.
EOC, *Model equal opportunity policy*, Manchester, EOC, 1988.
EOC, *Sex discrimination decisions*, Manchester, EOC (ongoing).

Equal Pay Act 1970, London, HMSO, 1970.
Etzioni, A., *A comparative analysis of complex organisations*, 2nd ed., New York, Free Press, 1975.
European management guides: Vol. 1: Recruitment; Vol. 2: Terms and conditions of employment; Vol. 3: Industrial relations; Vol. 4: Pay and benefits; Vol. 5: Training and development, London, Incomes Data Services and IPM, 1990–2.
Financing our public library service: four subjects for debate, London, HMSO, 1988 (Green Paper: Cm 324).
Fincham, R. and Rhodes, P. S., *The individual, work and organisation*, London, Weidenfeld & Nicholson, 1988.
Fisher, R. and Ury, W., *Getting to yes: negotiating agreements without giving in*, London, Arrow, 1987.
Fowler, A., *Effective negotiation*, London, IPM, 1986.
Fowler, A., *Getting off to a good start: successful employee induction*, London, IPM, 1987.
Fowler, A., 'New directions in performance pay', *Personnel management*, **20** (11), 1988, 30–4.
Fowler, A., *Personnel management in local government*, 2nd ed., London, IPM, 1980.
Fox, A., *Industrial sociology and industrial relations*, London, HMSO, 1966.
Further Education Unit, *Investing in change: an appraisal of staff development needs for the delivery of modernised occupational training*, London, FEU, 1986.
Further Education Unit, *Quality in NAFE*, London, FEU, 1987.
GMB, *The 1990's and beyond*, London, GMB, 1987. With section by John Edmonds.
Garratt, B., *The learning organization*, London, Fontana/Collins, 1987.
Garratt, B., *Management behaviour: individuals and groups*, Rugby, Action Learning Associates, 1980.
Gill, D. (ed.), *Indirect discrimination: the state of the law*, London, IPM, 1986.
Gill, D., *Statutory sick pay – the new rules*, London, IPM, 1985.
Gill, D. and Ungerson, B., *Equal pay – the challenge of equal value*, London, IPM, 1984.
Glucklich, P. and Snell, M., *Women, work and wages*, London, Low Pay Unit, 1982 (Discussion series No. 2).
Goodall, D. L., 'Performance measurement: a historical perspective', *Journal of librarianship*, **20** (2), 1988, 128–47.
Graham, C. and Lewis, N., *The role of ACAS conciliation in equal pay and discrimination*, Manchester, EOC, 1985.

Greater London Council. Equal Opportunities Group, *Challenging heterosexism in the work place*, London, GLC, 1986.

Greater London Employers' Secretariat, *Recruitment and retention of employees in London local government*, London, GLES, 1987–88 (GLES reports Nos. 1–3).

Greater London Joint Council for Craft and Trades Workers, Handbook, 4th ed., London, GLJCCTW, 1986 (*Green book*: updated each year).

Greater London Joint Council for Local Authorities Services (Manual Workers), Joint Secretariat, *Harmonisation and single status – joint GLJC guidelines*, London, GLJC, nd.

Greater London Joint Council for Local Authority Services (Manual Workers), *Schedule of wages and working conditions, and conditions, functions and recommendations of the Council*, London, GLJCLAS, 1977 (*Buff book*: updated each year).

Gregg, P. A. and Machin, S. J., 'Unions and the incidence of performance-linked pay schemes in Britain', *International journal of industrial organisations*, 6 (1), 1988, 91ff.

Gregory, J., 'Equal pay and sex discrimination: why women are giving up the fight, *Feminist review*, 75, 1982.

Gregory, J., *Sex, race and the law*, London, Sage, 1987.

Guyton, T., *Unionization: the viewpoint of librarians*, Chicago, American Library Association, 1975.

Hakin, C., *Occupational segregation: a comparative study of the degree and pattern of differentiation between men's and women's work*, London, Department of Employment (Research paper No. 9).

Hammond, V., 'Men and women managers: the challenge of working together', *Women and training news*, 5, 1981, 6–7.

Handy, C. B., *The making of managers*, London, MSC/NEDO/NEDQ, 1987.

Handy, C. B., *Understanding organisations*, 3rd ed., London, Penguin, 1985.

Harrison, M., 'Participation of women in trade union activities', *Industrial relations journal*, 10 (2), 1979, 41–55.

Herzberg, G., *The motivation to work*, London, 2nd ed., Chapman and Hall, 1959.

Hill, N. C., *Counselling at the workplace*, London, McGraw-Hill, 1981.

'How far has the company equality gone?', *Labour research*, 77 (12), 1989, 11–13.

Howells, B. and Barrett, B., *Health and Safety at Work Act: a guide for managers*, London, IPM, 1982.

Hunt, A. (ed.), *Women and paid work: issues of equality*, London, Macmillan, 1988.
Hunt, J. and Adams, S., 'Women, work and trade union organisations', *Studies for trade unionists*, 6 (21), 1980, complete issues.
Hurstfield, J., *The part-time trap*, London, Low Pay Unit, 1978 (Low pay pamphlet No. 9).
In place of strife: a policy for industrial relations, London, HMSO, 1969 (Cmnd 3888).
Incomes Data Services, *Contracts of employment*, London, IDS, 1987.
Incomes Data Services, *IDS employment law handbook No. 39: contracts of employment*, London, IDS, 1987.
Incomes Data Services, *The new race relations law and employment*, London, IDS, 1976.
Industrial relations in Britain: an Industrial Relations Services guide, London, Industrial Relations Services, 1988.
Industrial Society, *Notes for managers*, new ed., London, Industrial Society, 1989.
Information needs of trade unionists: the role of the public library: report of a seminar October 1985, Department of Information Studies, University of Sheffield, 1986 (CRUS working paper No. 8).
Institute of Personnel Management, *Staff status for all*, London, IPM, 1977.
Jackson, M., *Trade unions*, Harlow, Longmans, 1988.
Jobbins, D., 'Exercising the brain muscle', *Times higher education supplement*, 14 July 1979, 7.
Johnston, B., 'Industrial relations and the librarian', *Assistant librarian*, 76 (9), 1983, 114–16.
Jones, K., *Conflict and change in library organisations*, London, Bingley, 1984.
Kahn-Freund, O., *Labour relations and the law*, London, Stevens, 1965.
Kakabadse, A., *The politics of organisations*, Aldershot, Gower, 1984.
Karp, R. S., 'Public library unions: some questions', *Public library quarterly*, 8 (3/4), 1988, 73–80.
Katz, D. and Kahn, R. L., *Social psychology of organisations*, New York, Wiley, 1978.
Kedney, B. and Parkes, D. (eds.), *Planning the F. E. curriculum: implications of the 1988 Education Reform Act*, London, FEU, 1988.
Keine, R. and Mallaber, J., *Whose value? Whose money? How to assess the real value of council services*, London, TUC/Local Government Information Unit, 1986.

Kennedy, G., Benson, J. and McMillan, J., *Managing negotiations*, 2nd ed., London, Business Books, 1984.

Klein, M., *Our adult world and other essays*, London, Heinemann, 1963.

Labour and the unions, London, Conservative Research Department, 1989.

LAMSAC, *Putting performance review into practice*, London, Local Authorities Management Services and Computer Committee, 1979.

Land, H., *Parity begins at home: women's and men's work in the home and its effects on their paid employment: a research review*, Manchester, EOC, 1981.

Leadbetter, C., 'Divisions of labour', *Marxism today*, May 1988, 19-23.

Lear, T. E. (ed.), *Spheres of group analysis*, London, Group Analytic Society Publications, 1984.

Legal side of employing union members, London, Incomes Data Services, 1984.

Lewis, J. (ed.), *Women's welfare, women's rights*, London, Croom Helm, 1983.

Library Association (LA), *Duties and responsibilities of library staff in local authorities with grading recommendations*, London, LA, 1986.

LA, *Equal opportunities information pack*, London, LA, 1989.

LA, *National salary scales for civil service librarians*, London, LA, 1986.

LA, *Recommended salaries and conditions of service for library staff in colleges and polytechnics*, London, LA, 1986.

LA, *Recommended salaries for library staff in commercial, industrial and other specialised library and information services*, London, LA, 1984.

LA, *Recommended salary grades for library staff in the National Health Service*, London, LA, 1986.

Line, M. B. (ed.), *Academic library management*, London, Library Association Publishing, 1990.

Little, A. and Robbins, D., *Loading the law*, London, CRE, 1982.

Local Authorities Conditions of Service Advisory Board, *Equal opportunities and employment: a brief summary of the law*, London, LACSAB, 1985 (Employers Guide No. 102).

Local Authorities Conditions of Service Advisory Board, *Pay, conditions of service and industrial relations in local government: an employers' strategy*, London, LACSAB, 1987.

Local Government Act 1988, London, HMSO, 1988.

Local Government Finance Act, 1988, London, HMSO, 1988.

Local Government and Housing Act 1989, London, HMSO, 1989.

Local Government Campaign Unit, *Bearing the burden: women's work and local governments*, London, LGCU, 1985.

Local Government Training Board (LGTB), *Art of negotiation*, Luton, LGTB.

LGTB, *Employee relations in local government: a study guide*, Luton, LGTB, 1981.

LGTB, *Fair selection: recruitment and selection of staff and equal opportunities: a resource pack for trainers*, Luton, LGTB, 1986.

LGTB, *Improving local government employee relations: how are you managing?* Luton, LGTB, 1984.

LGTB, *Managers and industrial relations: the identification of training needs*, Luton, LGTB, 1983.

LGTB, *Managing industrial relations: trade union representation and local industrial relations machinery*, Luton, LGTB, 1986.

LGTB, *Performance review and staff development schemes and case history*, Luton, LGTB, 1986.

LGTB, *Practical guide to effective coaching: a manager's guide*, Luton, LGTB, 1988.

LGTB, *Problem solving and decision making for local government officers*, Luton, LGTB, 1983.

LGTB, *Safety and employee services*, Luton, LGTB, 1975.

Lovelady, L., 'Change strategies and the use of OD consultants to facilitate change, Part 1: Alternative change strategies reviewed', *Leadership and organisational development journal*, 5 (2), 1984, 3–10.

Lyth, I. M., *Containing anxiety in institutions*, London, Free Association Books, 1988.

McCann, D., *How to influence others at work: psychoverbal communication for managers*, London, Heinemann, 1988.

McDonald, I., *Race relations: the new law*, London, Butterworth, 1977.

McDonald, T. J. and Ward, S. K. (eds), *The politics of urban fiscal policy*, London, Sage, 1985.

McGregor, D., *The human side of enterprise*, New York, McGraw-Hill, 1960.

McMurran, M. and Cushway, D., 'Assertiveness at work', *Training and development*, 7 (7), 1988, 15, 16, 19.

Maidment, W. R., 'Trade unionism in public libraries', *Journal of librarianship*, 8, 1976, 143–52.

Management Charter Initiative, *Proposed national framework for management development*, London, CMED, 1988.

Managing colleges efficiently, London, HMSO, 1987.

Management of discipline: a training course, Sheffield, MSC, 1984.

Manpower Services Commission, *Code of good practice on the employment of disabled people*, rev. ed., Sheffield, MSC/CBI/TUC, 1987.

Marchington, M., 'The four faces of employee consultation', *Personnel management*, May 1988, 44-.

Margarison, C., *Influencing organisational change*, London, IPM, 1978.

Marris, P., *Loss and change*, London, Routledge and Kegan Paul, 1974.

Marsh, A., *Trade union handbook*, Aldershot, Gower, 1988.

Marsh, P. R., *White collar unionism in libraries*, Sheffield University Postgraduate School of Librarianship and Information Studies, 1980. (Occasional Publications No. 11).

Marshall, J., *Women managers: travellers in a male world*, Chichester, Wiley, 1984.

Martin, J. and Roberts, C., *Women and employment: a lifetime perspective*, London, Department of Employment/Office of Population Censuses and Surveys, 1984.

Menzies, I. E. P., *The functioning of social systems as a defence against anxiety*, London, Tavistock Institute of Human Relations, 1970.

Miller, J., *Towards a new psychology of women*, London, Penguin, 1976.

Milne, A. R., *Counselling at work*, Bromley, Centre for Professional Development Counselling, 1988 (Occasional Papers No. 2).

Mitter, S., *Common facts, common bond: women and the global economy*, London, Pluto, 1986.

Mullard, M., *The politics of public expenditure*, London, Croom Helm, 1987.

NALGO, *Fighting privatisation in local government: report of the National Local Government Committee*, London, NALGO, 1986.

NATFHE, *The NATFHE handbook*, Mansfield, Linneys, 1989.

National Joint Council for Further Education Lecturers in England and Wales, rev. ed., London, NJCFE, 1987 (*Silver book*: updated each year).

National Joint Council for Local Authorities Administrative, Professional, Technical and Clerical Services, *Scheme of conditions of service*, London, NJCLA, 1975 (*Purple book*).

National Joint Council for Local Authority Services (Manual workers), *Handbook*, rev. ed., London, NJCLAS, 1988 (*White book*).

Nichols, T. and Armstrong, P., *Workers divided*, London, Fontana, 1976.

Office of Arts and Libraries, *Keys to success: performance indicators for public libraries. A manual of performance measures and indicators* developed by King Research Ltd, London, HMSO, 1990 (Library Information Series No. 18).

Office of Manpower Studies, *Equal pay: first report on the implementation of the Equal Pay Act 1970*, London, HMSO, 1972.

O'Higgins, P., *Labour law in Great Britain and Ireland 1979-85: a bibliography*, London, Mansell, 1987.

O'Neill, P., *Information and trade unions: a report to the Commonwealth Relations Trust*, London, Trade Union Information Group, 1986.

O'Reilly, C. and O'Reilly, M. I., *Librarians and labour relations: employment under union contracts*, London, Greenwood Press, 1981.

Organising for the 1990s, London, TUC, 1989.

Palmer, C. and Poulton, K., *Sex and race discrimination in employment*, London, Legal Action Group, 1988.

Payne, D. (ed.), *Employment law manual*, Aldershot, Gower, (ongoing).

Peace, N. E., 'Personnel employment: collective bargaining', in *American Library Association yearbook*, Chicago, ALA, 1981, 219.

Pearson, C., 'For better, for worse: industrial relations and librarianship', *Assistant librarian*, 73 (12), 1980, 16, 63.

Pedler, M., *Action learning in practice*, Aldershot, Gower, 1983.

Personnel managers' year book 1989, London, AP Information Services, 1989.

Peters, T. J. and Waterman, J. H., *In search of excellence*, New York, Harper and Row, 1982.

Pollitt, C., 'Beyond the managerial model: the case for broadening performance assessment in government and the public services', *Financial accountability and management*, 2 (3), 1986, 155-70.

A problem shared, London, ACAS/MSC, 1988 (video).

Public service labour relations: recent trends and future prospects, Geneva, International Labour Office, 1987.

Purcell, J., *Good industrial relations: theory and practice*, London, Macmillan, 1981.

Racial discrimination: a guide to the Race Relations Act, London, HMSO, 1976.

Raddon, R., 'Question-time – public libraries, are they worth it? *Public library journal*, 3 (6), 1988, 113-17.

Reddy, M., 'Counselling in organisations', *Training officer*, 21 (8), 1985, 236-9.

Reddy, M., *The manager's guide to counselling at work*, London, Methuen, 1987.

Reed, B. D. and Palmer, B. W. M., *An introduction to organisational* behaviour, London, Grubb Institute of Behavioural Studies, 1972.

Removing barriers to employment: proposals for further reform of industrial relations and trade union law, London, HMSO, 1989 (Cm 655).

Report of the steering committee for efficiency studies in universities, London, Committee of Vice-Chancellors and Principals, 1985 (Jarratt Report).

Revans, R. W., *Action learning: new techniques for management*, London, Blond and Briggs, 1980.

Revans, R. W., *The response of the manager to change*, Chelmsford, Action Learning Trust, 1971.

Revill, D. H., *Personnel management in polytechnic libraries*, Aldershot, Gower, 1987.

Rice, A. K., *The enterprise and its environment*, London, Tavistock, 1963.

Richardson, E., *The teacher, the school and the task of management*, London, Heinemann Education, 1973.

Ritchie, S., 'Women in library management', in Vaughan, A. (ed.), *Studies in library management*, Vol. 7, London, Bingley, 1982, 13–36.

Robarts, S. and others, *Positive action for women: the next step*, Nottingham, Russell Press, 1981.

Roberts, C. (ed.), *Harmonisation: whys and wherefores*, London, IPM, 1985.

Roberts, N. and Konn, T., *Librarians and professional status*, London, Library Association Publishing, 1991.

Rooks, D. C., *Motivating today's library staff: a management guide*, London, Oryx, 1988.

Rosebeth, K. M., *The change masters*, London, Unwin, 1988.

Rosenthal, M., 'The impact of unions on salaries in public libraries', *Library quarterly*, 55 (1), January 1985, 52-70.

Rubenstein, M., *Discrimination: a guide to the relevant case law on race and sex discrimination and equal pay*, London, Industrial Relations Services, 1988.

Rubenstein, M. and Frost, Y., *Unfair dismissal: a guide to relevant case law*, 6th ed., London, Industrial Relations Services, 1988.

Ruse, D., 'What now?: the future without the librarian's grade', *Library Association record*, 86 (8), 1984, 305.

Salzberger-Wittenberg, I., *Psycho-analytical insight and relationships*, London, Routledge and Kegan Paul, 1970.

Sashkin, M., *Making participative management work*, Carmarthen, Management Learning Resources, 1988.

Sex Discrimination Act 1975, London, HMSO, 1975 (Amendment 1986).

Shields, M., 'Trades unionists: a new challenge to library education', *Education libraries bulletein*, 26 (1), 1983, 39–43.

Slaikev, K. and others, 'Manning the psychological first aid posts', *Management today*, February 1986, 35–6.

Smart, C., 'Information in industrial relations', *Aslib proceedings*, 321 (7/8), 1980, 302–9.

Smith, P. B. (ed.), *Small groups and personal change*, London, Methuen, 1980.

Society of Personnel Officers, *Monitoring an equal opportunity policy*, London, SOCPO, 1985.

Soltow, A. J., 'University industrial relations in libraries: an overview', *Special libraries*, 67 (4), 1976, 195–201.

Special Review Body, First Report, London, TUC, 1988.

Spicer, R. (ed.), *Employment case law index*, Kingston, Kluwer Publishing, 1987.

Stephenson, J., 'Ineffective tribunals', *New society*, 29 April 1988, 23–5.

Stewart, J., *Local government: the conditions of local choice*, London, Allen and Unwin for Institute of Local Government Studies, 1983.

Stewart, R., *The reality of management*, London, Heinemann, 1963.

Storr, A., *The art of psychotherapy*, London, Secker and Warburg, 1979.

Streamlining the cities: government proposals for reorganising the metropolitan counties, London, HMSO, 1983 (Cmnd. 9063).

Stuart, C. and Rosehay, S., 'Partnership creates centre for union studies', *Library Association record*, 80 (3), 1978, 118–9.

Swap, W. C. and others, *Group decision making*, London, Sage Publications, 1984.

Syrett, M., *Employing job sharers, part time and temporary staff*, London, IPM, 1983.

Taylor, B. and Lippett, G. (eds.), *Management development and training handbook*, London, McGraw-Hill, 1983.

Taylor, R., *The fifth estate: Britain's unions in the modern world*, rev. ed., London, Pan Books, 1980.

Taylor, R. D., 'Trade unions and librarianship', in Holroyd, D. (ed.), *Studies in library management*, vol. 4, London, Bingley, 1977.

Thomas, R. R., 'From affirmative action to affirming diversity', *Harvard business review*, 68 (2), 1990, 107–17.

Thomason, G., *Textbook of industrial relations management*, London, Institute of Personnel Management, 1984.

Todd, K., 'Collective bargaining and professional associations in the library field', *Library quarterly*, 55 (3), 1985, 284–99.
Tolley's employment handbook, London, Tolley, 1986.
Tomkins, C. R., *Achieving economy, efficiency and effectiveness in the public sector*, Routledge and Kegan Paul, 1987.
Trade union immunities, London, HMSO, 1981 (Cmnd. 8128).
Trade unions and their members, London, HMSO, 1988 (*Green paper*).
Trades Union Congress (TUC), *Bargaining in privatised companies*, London, TUC, 1986.
Travers, T., *The politics of local government finance*, London, Allen and Unwin, 1986.
TUC, *Black and ethnic-minority women in employment and trade unions*, London, TUC, 1987.
TUC, *Black workers' charter*, London, TUC, 1987.
TUC, *Contract compliance and equal opportunities*, London, TUC, 1986.
TUC, *Disputes: principles and procedures*, rev. ed., London, TUC, 1988.
TUC, *Education and training of girls and women*, London, TUC, 1987.
TUC, *Equal pay for work of equal value*, London, TUC, 1984.
TUC, *Equality for women within trades unions*, London, TUC, 1984.
TUC, *Employment and technology*, London, TUC, 1979.
TUC, *Fair wages strategy: national minimum wage*, London, TUC, 1986.
TUC, *Guide to the Employment Bill*, London, TUC, 1987.
TUC, *Health and safety at work: a TUC guide*, London, TUC, 1975.
TUC, *Industrial democracy*, London, TUC, 1974.
TUC, *Images of inequality*, London, TUC, 1984.
TUC, *Industrial relations legislation*, London, TUC, 1986.
TUC, *New technology – the chip at work*, London, TUC, 1984.
TUC, *Positive action programmes*, London, TUC, 1986.
TUC, *Privatisation by order*, London, TUC, 1985.
TUC, *Sexual harrassment at work*, London, TUC, 1983.
TUC, *Trade unions and black workers*, London, TUC, 1986.
TUC, *Trade unions and multinational companies*, London, TUC, 1984.
TUC, *TUC guidelines on VDUs*, London, TUC, 1985.
TUC, *Wages councils*, London, TUC, 1985.
TUC, *Women and new technology*, London, TUC, 1984.
TUC, *Women in the labour market*, London, TUC, 1983.
TUC, *Women's health at risk*, London, TUC, 1986.
TUC, *Working women*, London, TUC, 1983.

TUC, *Workplace health and safety services*, London, TUC, 1981.
Training Commission, *Classifying the components of management competancies*, London, Training Commission, 1988.
Walby, S., *General segregation at work*, Milton Keynes, Open University, 1988.
Walker, A. and Walker, C., *The growing divide*, London, Child Poverty Action Group, 1987.
Walton, F. (ed.), *New encyclopaedia of employment law and practice*, London, Centurion Publications, 1985.
Weber, M., *Theory of social and economic organization*, Glencoe, Free Press, 1947.
Wedderburn, K. W., *The worker and the law*, London, Penguin, 1971.
Whitaker, D. S., *Using groups to help people*, London, Routledge and Kegan Paul, 1985.
Widdicombe, D., *The conduct of local authority business: report of the committee of inquiry*, London, HMSO, 1986 (Cmnd. 9797–9801).
Wilkinson, T., *Guide to workplace ballots*, London, IPM, 1987.
Williams, R., 'Labour history and the local studies library', *Local studies librarian*, 3 (1), 1984, 26–7.
Winkworth, I., *Library staff and trade unionism: a study of attitudes and attitudes and influences*, MPhil dissertation, University of Durham, 1986.
Winnicott, D. W., *The family and individual development*, London, Tavistock, 1965.
Winnicott, D. W., *Maturational processes and the facilitating environment*, London, Hogarth Press, 1972.
Winning a fair deal for women: a GMB policy for equality, London, GMB (no date).
Winterton, I. and Winterton, R., *New technology: the bargaining issues*, London, IPM, 1985 (Occasional papers in industrial relations No. 7).
Work Research Unit, *Information system bibliographies, No. 46: Performance appraisal*, London, Work Research Unit, 1988.
Young, F., *Employment and law handbook*, Aldershot, Gower, 1987.

18 Journals

ASLIB proceedings, London, Aslib (monthly).
ACAS library bulletin, London, ACAS (monthly).
British journal of industrial relations, Oxford, Basil Blackwell Ltd (3 per annum: March, July and November).
Bulletin of labour statistics, London, ILO (quarterly).

Bibliography 143

CBI news (Confederation of British Industry), London, CBI (fortnightly).
Conditions of work digest, Geneva, ILPO (bi-annual).
Counselling news for managers, Bromley, Centre for Professional Employment Counselling (irregular).
Croner's employment digest, Kingston, Croner Publications Ltd (22 per year).
Employment bulletin and IR digest, Bradford, MCB University Press (monthly).
Employment gazette, London, HMSO (monthly).
Employment news, London, Department of Employment (monthly).
Employment report, London, Commission for Racial Equality (quarterly).
Employee counselling today, 4/5 issues per year. Bradford, MCB University Press.
Employee relations, Bradford, MCB University Press (bi-monthly).
Equal opportunities review, London, Eclipse Publications (bi-monthly).
European industrial relations review, London, Eclipse Publications (monthly).
Financial statistics, London, HMSO (monthly).
Halsbury's laws of English monthly reviews, London, Butterworth (monthly).
Harvard business review, Boston, Harard University Graduate School of Business Administration (bi-monthly).
Health and safety information bulletin, London, Eclipse (monthly).
Human resource management, New York, John Wiley & Sons Inc. (quarterly).
Industrial relations journal, Oxford, Basil Blackwell Ltd (quarterly).
Industrial relations law reports, London, Eclipse Publications (monthly).
International journal of quality and reliability management, 6 issues per year. Bradford, MCB University Press.
International labour reports, Barnsley, Mayday Publications (bi-monthly).
International labour review, Geneva, International Labour Office (bi-monthly).
Journal of European industrial training, Bradford, MCB University Press (8 per annum).
Journal of industrial relations, Sydney, Australia, Industrial Relations Society of Australia (quarterly).
Journal of librarianship, London, Library Association (quarterly).
Library Association record, London, Library Association (monthly).

Local government chronicle, London, Brown, Knight & Truscott Ltd (weekly).
Local government trends, London, CIPFA (annual).
Management today, London, Management Publications Ltd (monthly).
Management training and development, Luton, Local Government Training Board (2 per annum).
Marxism today, London, Communist Party of Great Britain (monthly).
Municipal journal, London, Municipal Journal Ltd (weekly).
New statesman and society, London, Statesman & Nation Publishing Co Ltd (weekly).
Journal of occupational psychology, Leicester, British Psychological Society (quarterly).
Pay and benefits bulletin, London, Eclipse Publications (fortnightly).
Personnel management, London, Personnel Publications Ltd (monthly)
Personnel training and education, London, Library Association, Personnel Training and Education Group (3 per annum).
Political quarterly, Oxford, Basil Blackwell (quarterly).
Privatisation news, London, Local Government Privatisation Research Unit (10 per annum).
Public library journal, London, Library Association, Public Libraries Group (bi-monthly).
Race and class, London, Institute of Race Relations (quarterly).
Social intelligence, London, Taylor Graham Publishing (3 per annum).
Strategic management journal, Chichester, John Wiley & Sons (bi-monthly).
Studies for trade unionists, London, WEA (4 per annum).
Trade union news, London, Library Association (irregular).
Training and development, Marlow, ITD Journals Ltd (monthly).
TUC bulletin, London, TUC (10 per annum).
Women and training news, Gloucester, Training Agency (quarterly).
Women at work, Geneva, International Labour Office (2 per annum).
Work, employment and society, Solihull, BSA Publications Ltd, London, British Sociological Association (quarterly).

19 Organizations

ACAS (Advisory, Conciliation and Arbitration Service), Clifton House, 83–117 Euston Road, London NW1 2RB.
Action Learning Associates, 83 Bilton Road, Rugby, Warwick CV22 7AE.

Action Learning Trust, Anglian Regional Management Centre, Danbury Park, Danbury, Chelmsford, Essex CM3 4AT.
Adam Smith Institute, 2 Abbey Orchard Street, London SW1P 2JH.
Aslib (Association for Information Management), 20–24 Old Street, London EC1V 9AP.
Association for the Development of Adult Political Education, 16 Gower Street, London WC1E 6DP.
Association of County Councils, 66a Eaton Square, London SW1 9BH.
Association of London Authorities, 36 Old Queen Street, London SW1H 9JF.
Association of Metropolitan Authorities, 36 Great Smith Street, London SW1P 3BJ.
Association of University Teachers, United House, 1 Pembridge Road, London W11.
Audit Commission, 1 Vincent Square, London SW1P 2PN.
BACIE (British Association for Commercial and Industrial Education), 16 Park Crescent, London W1N 4AP.
Birmingham Trade Union Resource Centre Ltd, Victoria Works, Frederick Street, Birmingham B1 3HE.
Bradford Resource Centre, 31 Manor Row, Bradford, West Yorks BD1 4PS.
Brent Local Economy Resource Unit, 389 High Street, Willesden, London NW10 2JR.
British Association for Counselling, 37a Sheep Street, Rugby, Warwickshire CV21 3BX.
British Institute of Management, Management House, Cottingham Road, Corby, Northants NN17 1TT.
Camden Trade Union Support Unit, 213 Eversholt Street, London NW1 1DB.
Campaign for Press and Broadcasting Freedom, 96 Dalston Lane, London E8 1NG.
Central Arbitration Committee, 39 Grosvenor Place, London SW1X 7BD.
Central London Law Centre, 13 Ingestre Place, London W1R 3LP.
Central Office of Industrial Tribunals, 93 Ebury Bridge Road, London SW1W 8RE.
Centre for Alternative Industrial and Technological Systems, Polytechnic of North London, Holloway Road, London N7 8DB.
Centre for Policy Research, 6 Duke of York Street, London SW1Y 6LA.

People and work

Centre for Professional Employment Counselling, Kent House, 41 East Street, Bromley, Kent BR1 1QQ.
Centre for Policy Studies, 8 Wilfred Street, London SW1E 6PL.
Centre for Trade Union Studies (SE Region), South Bank Polytechnic, Borough Road, London SE1 0AA.
Central Statistical Office, Great George Street, London SW1P 3AQ.
Certification Office, 15–17 Ormond Yard, Duke of York Street, London SW1Y 6JT.
Child Poverty Action Group, 1–5 Bath Street, London EC1V 9QQ.
City Centre (Resource Centre for Workers), 4th Floor, Sophia House, 32–5 Featherstone Street, London EC1Y 8QX.
Commission for Racial Equality, Elliot House, 10 Allington Street, London SW1E 5EH.
Commission of the European Communities, 8 Storeys Gate, London SW1P 3AT.
Commissioner for the Rights of Trade Union Members, First Floor, Bank Chambers, 2A Rylands Street, Warrington, Cheshire WA1 1EN.
Commonwealth Trade Union Council, Congress House, Great Russell Street, London WC1 3LS.
Confederation of British Industry, Centre Point, 103 New Oxford Street, London WC1A 1DU.
Council for Management Education and Development (CMED), Room 996, Shell UK Ltd, Shell-Mex House, Strand, London WC2R 0DX.
Council of Local Education Authorities, Eaton House, Eaton Square, London SW1W 9BH.
Department of Education and Science, Elizabeth House, York Road, London SE1 7PH.
Department of Employment, Library, Steel House, Tothill Street, London SW1H 9NF.
Department of Trade and Industry, 1–19 Victoria Street, London SW1H 0ET.
Employment and Trade Union Information Services, Central Library, Snow Hill, Wolverhampton WV1 3AX.
Employment Appeal Tribunal, 4 St James's Square, London SW1 4JU.
Employment Relations Associates, 80 Newmarket Road, Cambridge CB5 8DZ.
Employment Service, 236 Grays Inn Road, London WC1X 8HL.
Equal Opportunities Commission, Overseas House, Quay Street, Manchester M3 3HN.

Ergonomics Society, Gothic House, Barker Gate, Nottingham NG1 1JU.
European Foundation for Management Development, 40 Rue Washington, B-1050 Brussels, Belgium.
European Trade Union Confederation, Rue Montagne aux Herbes Potageres 37, 1000 Brussels, Belgium.
European Trade Union Institute, Boulevard de l'Imperatrice 66 (Bte 4), 1000 Brussels, Belgium.
Freedom Association, 11 Grape Street, London WC2H 8ET.
Further Education Staff College, Coombe Lodge, Blagdon, Bristol BS18 6RG.
GMB, 22–4 Worple Road, Wimbledon, London SW19 4DD.
General Federation of Trade Unions, Central House, Upper Woburn Place, London WC1H 0HY.
Greater London Employers' Secretariat, 4th Floor, Victoria Station House, 191 Victoria Street, London SW1E 5NE.
Greater London Enterprise Board, Spencer House, Newington Causeway, London SE1 6BD.
Grubb Institute of Behavioural Studies, The EWR Centre, Cloudesley Street, London N1 0HU.
Hackney Trades Union Support Unit, 489 Kingsland Road, London E8 4AU.
Haldane Society, Room 205, Panther House, 38 Mount Pleasant, London WC1X 0AP.
Health and Safety Executive, Baynards House, 1–13 Chepstow Place, London W2 4TF.
Incomes Data Services Ltd, 193 St John Street, London EC1V 4LS.
Industrial Participation Association, 85 Tooley Street, London SE1 2QZ.
Industrial Relations Services, 18–20 Highbury Place, London N5 1QP.
Industrial Society, Robert Hyde House, 48 Bryanston Square, London W1H 1BQ.
Industrial Tribunals (Central Office), 93 Ebury Bridge Road, London SW1W 8RE.
Institute for Policy Research, 8 Wilfred Street, London SW1E 6PL.
Institute of Group Analysis, 1 Daleham Gardens, London NW3 5BY.
Institute of Information Scientists, 44 Museum Street, London WC1A 1LY.
Institute of Manpower Studies, Mantell Building, University of Sussex, Falmer, Brighton BN1 9RF.

Institute of Personnel Management, IPM House, Camp Road, London SW19 4UW.
Institute of Training and Development, Meadow House, Institute Road, Marlow, Bucks SL7 1BN.
International Confederation of Free Trade Unions, Rue Montagne aux Herbes Potageres 37, 1000 Brussels, Belgium.
International Labour Office, 4 Route des Morillous CH-1211, Geneva, Switzerland; and Vincent House, Vincent Square, London SW1P 2NB.
International Organisation of Employers, 278 Chemin de Joinville, 1216 Cointrin, Geneva, Switzerland.
Irish Congress of Trade Unions, Congress House, 19 Raglan Road, Dublin 4, Eire.
Jim Conway Foundation, c/o Brunel University, Cleveland Road, Uxbridge, Middlesex UB8 3PH.
Labour Party Library, 150 Walworth Road, London SE17 1JT.
Labour Research Department, 78 Blackfriars Road, London SE1 8HF.
Lambeth Trade Union Resource Centre, Unit 117, Bon Marche Building, 444 Brixton Road, London SW9 8EJ.
Liberty – National Council for Civil Liberties, 21 Tabard Street, London SE1 4LA.
Library Association, 7 Ridgmount Street, London WC1E 7AE.
Local Authorities Conditions of Service Advisory Board (LACSAB) (now Local Government Management Board).
Local Government Information Unit, 1–5 Bath Street, London EC1V 9QQ.
Local Government Management Board, 41 Belgrave Square, London SW1 8NZ *and* Arndale House, The Arndale Centre, Luton LU1 2TS.
Local Government Training Board (now Local Government Management Board).
London University, Centre for Extra-Mural Studies, 26 Russell Square, London WC1B 5DQ.
Low Pay Unit, 9 Upper Berkeley Street, London W1H 8BY.
Manchester Employment Research Group, Room 37, Cavendish Building, Manchester Polytechnic, Manchester M15 6BG.
Marx Memorial Library, 37a Clerkenwell Green, London EC1R 0DU.
Merseyside Trade Union Community and Unemployed Resource Centre, 24 Hardman Street, Liverpool L1 9AX.
Migrant Services Unit, 68 Charlton Street, London NW1 1JR.
National and Local Government Officers' Association, 1 Mabledon Place, London WC1H 9AJ.

National Association of Teachers in Further and Higher Education, 27 Brittania Street, London WC1X 9JP.
National Council for Civil Liberties *see* Liberty.
National Council for Educational Technology, 3 Devonshire Street, London W1N 2BA.
National Economic Development Council, Millbank Tower, Millbank, London SW1P 4QX.
National Joint Council for Local Authorities Services (Work people), Employers' Side Secretary – D. E. Thomas, 41 Belgrave Square, London SW1X 8NZ.
National Joint Council for Local Authorities Services (Administrative, Professional, Technical and Clerical Services), Staff Side Secretary – Keith Sonnett, NALGO, 1 Mabledon Place, London WC1H 9AJ.
National Joint Council for Local Authorities Services (Work people), Trade Union Secretary – D. McGregor, GMB, 22–4 Worple Road, Wimbledon, London SW19 4DD.
National Museum of Labour History, 103 Princess Street, Manchester M2 6DD.
National Society of Quality Circles, 2 Castle Street, Salisbury SP1 1BB.
North East Trade Union Studies Information Unit (TUSIU), Southend, Fernwood Road, Jesmond, Newcastle upon Tyne NE2 1TJ.
Nottingham 118 Workshop, 118 Mansfield Road, Nottingham NG1 3HL.
Organization for Economic and Cultural Development, 2 Rue Andre Pascal, 75 775 Paris Cedex 16, France.
Office of Wages Councils, Steel House, Tothill Street, London SE1H 9NF.
Open University, Walton Hall, Milton Keynes MK7 6AA.
Policy Studies Institute, 100 Park Village East, London NE1 3SR.
Polytechnics and Colleges Funding Committee, Metropolis House, 22 Percy Street, London W1P 9FF.
Royal Institute of Public Administration, 3 Birdcage Walk, London SW1H 9JH.
Runnymead Trust, 174 North Gower Street, London NW1.
School for Advanced Urban Studies, Rodney Lodge, Grange Road, Clifton, Bristol BS8 4EA.
Service Workers Action and Advisory Project, Room 160, South Bank House, Black Prince Road, London SE1 7SJ.
Services to Community Action and Trade Unionists, 15 Micawber Street, London N1 7TB.

Society of Chief Personnel Officers, Charnwood Borough Council, Southfields, Loughborough, Leics LE11 9TX.
Southall Trade Union Employment Advisory Service, 14 Featherstone Road, Southall, Middlesex UB2 5AA.
Southwark Trade Union Support Unit, 42 Braganza Street, London SE17 3RJ.
Tavistock Clinic (Training Office), Tavistock Centre, 120 Belsize Lane, London NW3 5BA.
Tom Mann Centre, Central Library, Southford Way, Coventry CV1 1FY.
Tower Hamlets International Solidarity, Oxford House, Derbyshire Street, Bethnal Green, London E2 6HG.
Trade Union Information Group, 112 Thorold Road, Ilford, Esex IG1 4EY.
Trade Union Studies Information Unit, Southenbd, Fernwood Road, Jesmond, Newcastle upon Tyne NE2 1TJ.
Trade Union International Research and Education Group, Ruskin College, Walton Street, Oxford OX1 2HE.
Trade Union Studies Unit, Sandwell College of Further and Higher Education, Pound Road, Oldbury, Sandwell, West Midlands B68 8NA.
Trades Union Congress, Congress House, 23–8 Great Russell Street, London WC1B 3LS.
Training Agency (now Training Enterprise and Education Directorate).
Training Enterprise and Education Directorate, Moorfoot, Sheffield S1 4PQ.
Transnationals Information Centre London, 9 Poland Street, London W1V 3DG.
Union of Industrial and Employers Confederation of Europe, Department of Information, Rue Joseph II 40 (Bre 4), 1040 Brussels, Belgium.
Waltham Forest Trade Union Resource Centre, YESS Project Building, Markhouse Road, Walthamstow, London E17 8BD.
Wolverhampton Trade Union Education Centre, Education Centre, Springvale House, Millfields Road, Bilston Wolverhampton WV14 0QS.
Work Research Unit, 27 Wilton Street, London SW1X 7AZ.
Workbase TU Education and Skills Project, Manbey School, Coopers Road, London SE1 5EA.
World Federation of Trade Unions, Vinohrad ska 10, 12147 Prague 2, Czechoslovakia.

20 Training resources

Appraising performance appraisal, LGTB, 1987 (pack).
Are you really helping?, Bromley, CEPEC, 1998 (video).
Case studies in industrial relations training, Cambridge, Employment Relations, 1987 (case studies).
Collective bargaining, Sheffield, MSC, 1983 (multi-media programme).
Course directory 1989, London, Industrial Society, 1989 (training resources directory).
Essential of health and safety at work, London, HMSO for Health and Safety Executive, 1988 (information booklet).
Effective manager, Milton Keynes, Open University, 1989 (course).
Everything is negotiable, Peterborough, Guild Sound and Vision, 1987 (video).
Face to face, Peterborough, Guild Sound and Vision, 1973 (video).
Fair selection: recruitment and selection of staff and equal opportunities, Luton, LGTB, 1986 (training pack).
Getting to work, Cambridge, Employment Relations (video).
Getting to grips with training, Luton, LGTB, 1987 (training pack).
Gone today, here tomorrow, Peterborough, Guild Sound and Vision, 1986 (video).
Improving communication and consultation: a course for local government managers and supervisors, Luton, LGTB, 1986 (training pack).
Improving local government employee relations – how are you managing?, Luton, LGTB, 1986 (training pack).
Industrial relations and the supervisor, Cambridge, Employment Relations (manual).
Industrial society training initiative: information pack 1, London, Industrial Society, 1988 (training pack).
Initiatives in training and development No.1: Training for change, London, Industrial Society, 1989 (training pack).
Management of discipline, Sheffield, MSC, 1984 (training pack).
Management training directory 1989/90, London, Task Force Pro Libra, 1989.
Managers and industrial relations, Cambridge, Employment Relations (manual).
Managers and industrial relations: the identification of training needs, Luton, LGTB, 1987 (pack).
Management of discipline and grievance handling, Luton, LGTB, 1986 (training pack).

Managing industrial relations – trade union representation and local industrial relations machinery, Luton, LGTB, 1986 (training resource materials).
Managing people, Milton Keynes, Open University, 1989 (course).
Panel interviews, Luton, LGTB, 1987 (video).
People at work, Sheffield, MSC, 1982 (training programme).
Performance appraisal survey, Luton, LGTB, 1986 (survey).
Performance review and staff development scheme, Luton, LGTB, 1986 (case history).
Personnel management and industrial relations, Luton, LGTB, 1989 (training package).
Politics of local government: implications for management development, Luton, LGTB, 1984 (discussion papers).
Problem shared, London, ACAS/MSC, 1988 (video).
What can you do?, Luton, LGTB, 1987 (video).
Where's the trust?, Peterborough, Guild Sound and Vision, 1975 (video).
Why trade unions?, London, Team Video Productions, 1988 (video).
Women into management, Milton Keynes, Open University, 1989 (course).
Working with trade unions, Sheffield, MSC, 1984 (video).

21 Legislation

Employment law and legislation is a complex area, constantly changing as new legislation is implemented, and with a wealth of case studies. It must also be seen in the context of changing political ideologies as legislation reflects current shifts in thinking. This is an important element, as trade unionism and employment law have a strong relationship, which derives from the tensions between employers and employees, and the need for both to protect their interests. These interests may have, and still do, clash, and changes in legislation reflect these tensions. Changes are still being planned and reflect further tensions – that is those between Governments. The United Kingdom is anxious to confine potential industrial action still further, and is opposing the general support for 'the right to strike' currently under consideration by the European Community. Developing patterns and styles of management also reflect legislative changes.

Within the scope of this publication, it is not intended to provide a detailed guide to the legal situation, but rather a general framework within which the major pieces of legislation can be considered. Practitioners will rarely, if ever, be called upon to implement and enforce the legislation in isolation and would be supported by experts from the relevant departments.

As with every other aspect of managing human relations, an understanding of some of the control mechanisms is essential, and in the case of legal enforcement, it is necessary to understand the boundaries between expertise and subject interest. The following is a brief guide to some of the major pieces of British legislation indicating where managers may need further support.

Combination Acts 1799 and 1880
Both concerned with preventing workers meeting to discuss conditions of employment. Intended to maintain the social and economic status quo, which was bound up with the class structure.

Combination Acts 1824 and 1825
Beginning of the recognition of the right to 'associate'. Previous activities of workers meeting to discuss their conditions of employment had been seen as detrimental to the concept of free trade, as in the 1880 Act.

Combination Acts 1871 and 1876
Contained guidelines for the establishment of a Trades Union and established parameters for this.

Trade Disputes Act 1906
Extended collective rights including the right to strike.

Trade Union Act 1913
Defines objects and powers of trade unions. Concerned with the operation and scope of political funds.

Trade Union Act 1927
Designed to limit the potential damage caused by strikes, through restricting their legality to specific issues. The closed shop concept was no longer permitted. Determined that payment of a political levy should be voluntary. Reversed by the Trades Disputes and Trade Union Act 1946.

Hours of Employment Act 1936
Laid down conditions relating to the hours which women could work, and also some areas of work (such as night shifts) which excluded women. Repealed in 1988.

Disabled Persons Employment Acts 1944 and 1958
Intended to support the employment of people with disabilities. Still

very limited, as illustrated by the statistics.

Trade Disputes and Trade Unions Act 1946
Repealed the Trade Disputes and Trade Unions Act 1927 and restored the status of Trade Unions to their pre-1927 status.

Offices, Shops and Railway Premises Act 1963
Conditions of work including hygiene, and health and safety.

Industrial Training Act 1964
Includes definitions of vocational training and is intended to prevent discrimination in terms of facilities or services.

Trade Unions (Amalgamation) Act 1964
Lays down rules for balloting in relation to mergers, and also the legal requirements governing any change of name of unions.

Redundancy Payments Act 1965
Provided employees who were dismissed with financial compensation.

Employers Liability (Compulsory Insurance) Act 1969

Equal Pay Acts 1970 and 1975
Concerned with the exclusion of discrimination in relation to pay and some contracts of service. Also concerned with discrimination in relation to collective agreements and trade union practices. Some areas excluded and covered by other legislation. The Acts are concerned with the provision of equal pay for a man and a woman carrying out work which is of equal value. Amended in 1983, the provision was intended for equal pay for jobs which make similar but different demands on employees. This was done through the Equal Pay (Amendment) Regulations 1983.

Industrial Relations Act 1971
Complex and far-reaching piece of legislation concerned with establishing national procedures to deal with strikes and disputes, including the setting up of the National Industrial Relations Court. Also concerned with the control of the closed shop and with the enforcement of a series of industrial practices which were basically concerned with controlling ad hoc union activities and disputes, and the individual involved in industrial action. Removed legal support for pre-entry closed shop. Most of the powers were reversed by the Trade Union and Labour Relations Act 1974. Part of a major

series of laws concerned with generally restructuring union activities, and includes a 'Code of practice of industrial relations'.

Employment and Training Act 1973

Section 2 is the pertinent section and is concerned with providing training and support in relation to employment opportunities. Discrimination in this support or the provision of facilities is illegal.

Health and Safety at Work Act 1974

A comprehensive piece of legislation enforced by the Health and Safety Executive, aimed at protecting the health, safety and welfare of those defined within the legal category of 'workers'. There are specific applications for particular areas, such as mines and quarries, offices and shops, etc. The Act tries to encompass the needs of both employers and employees.

Trade Union and Labour Relations Acts 1974 and 1976

Repealed Industrial Relations Act 1971, but re-enacts some of the provisions of that Act, especially unfair dismissal. Includes the right to complain to an industrial tribunal in the case of unfair dismissal. Act makes it unfair for an employee to be dismissed for being a member or taking part in union activities. Abolished the National Industrial Relations Court, the Commission on Industrial Relations and the Registry of Trade Unions and Employers Associations.

Intended to provide some protection or immunities for workers involved in action which was furthering a union dispute. Outlines areas of immunity and liability. Defines the union membership agreement known as the 'closed shop', as well as defining 'collective agreement'. Also intended to prevent discrimination on grounds of gender or creed.

Employment Protection Act 1975

Changed some of the power of the 1971 Industrial Relations Act including transferring power to ACAS (Advisory, Conciliation and Arbitration Service). Concerned with guidance on disciplinary rules and procedures. Linked to the Health and Safety at Work Act. Also provides support for individual workers over conditions of service, including the provision of maternity pay and protection against dismissal on grounds of pregnancy. Supports unions in terms of recognition, consultation and information, and a structure for union activities was also formalized, such as allowing time off for union activities etc. Basically concerned with employment protection for all employees. Set up Central Arbitration Committee, concerned with collective rights in the workplace.

Rehabilitation of Offenders Act 1975
In general is intended to ensure that anyone imprisoned for a sentence of not more than 2½ years does not have the stigma of the conviction attached to them thereafter.

Sex Discrimination Act 1975
Seminal pieces of legislation which established the Equal Opportunities Commission.

Race Relations Act 1976
Repealed Race Relations Acts of 1965 and 1968. The Commission for Racial Equality, previously the Race Relations Board, was established by the Act and has a code of practice for employers. This Act is intended to prevent discrimination and ensure equality of treatment. Discrimination is unlawful on grounds of colour, race, nationality, ethnic or national origins. The Act defines direct and indirect discrimination, and is particularly concerned with areas of employment, including pay and contracts, plus education. It also defines 'racial group' and 'racial grounds'. It also covers training, housing and the provision of goods and services. Exceptions are limited. Discrimination tends to operate particularly against women and black workers and the concept of indirect discrimination has been a powerful weapon in the effort to reduce unfair practices. This relates to specifying conditions and practices which are not essential to employment and which can discriminate heavily against women or black workers. The case law is extensive. Includes the rights of individuals to bring cases to an Industrial Tribunal. The Act has strong links with the Sex Discrimination Act 1986, as both have their origins in areas of work and industrial relations which perpetuated social class, gender and racial discrimination. Again, the statistics illustrate that the position of black workers, despite the legislation and some equal opportunities policies, harmonization policies and contract compliance policies, is not in general equal to that of white male workers. There are links with the Sex Discrimination Act 1986, in that positive discrimination is illegal, but positive action can include training schemes and other devices to help eliminate the imbalance between black and white workers.

Employment Protection (Consolidation) Act 1978
Defines areas of unfair dismissal, including dismissal relating to union membership and dismissal on the grounds of pregnancy; also for time off for union activities.

Wages Councils Acts 1979
Established wages councils to determine pay and conditions of employment for specific workers.

Employment Act 1980
Major piece of legislation. Contains amendments to the above. Further amendments in the Employment Act 1982. Gives employers a choice of recognition to unions. Also concerned with limiting primary industrial action, including picketing through financial and organizational means. Some government funding available for the organization of balloting through the powers of the certification officer. He or she is enabled to refund some of the costs incurred in balloting. Also deals with restricting industrial action and political strikes (those not concerned directly with pay and conditions of service). Protection given to individuals not involved in union activities.

Employment Act 1982
Must be considered in conjunction with the 1980 Act, and is also intended to restrict union activity. Narrowed the grounds on which a union could lawfully organize a strike which was concerned with terms and conditions of work or employment. Outlined major differences between primary issues involving strike action, and secondary issues, which can be related to political changes manifested in legislative changes. Privatization and the Dock Labour Scheme are two such examples. Legal action can be taken against unions if strike action is considered to be held unlawful by the courts. Also included changes in the closed-shop legislation, with increased protection for workers and companies employing non-union labour. Ballot to be held by unions to retain post-entry closed shop. Defines more closely some of the terminology defined in the Trade Union and Labour Relations Act of 1970. Requires larger companies (over 250) to indicate how employees are given information relevant to them.

Local Government Finance Act 1982
Changed the provisions relating to the determining of the Block Grant. Established the Audit Commission.

Trade Union Act 1984
Considered in conjunction with the Employment Acts of 1980 and 1982. Concerned with maintaining a balance in trade union recognition, and procedures including collective bargaining. It was perceived by the government as protecting members from over-zealous

union decision making. Also includes guidelines for the democratization and organization of union activity. Includes secret ballots, secondary picketing, election of union committees, the collection of union dues by employers and with limiting strike activities.

Sex Discrimination Act (Amendment 1986)
The Equal Opportunities Commission and its Codes of Practice were enabled through this legislation. Concerned with the implementation of rights and the prevention of discrimination against male and female workers. The Acts are intended to prevent unlawful discrimination, either directly or indirectly, to full or part-time workers, self-employed people and contract workers. Direct discrimination involves treating a woman in a way differently from a man, as a direct result of her sex. Indirect discrimination involves conditions which mean that women are disadvantaged because of those conditions. The Act also applies to discrimination in training opportunities, and in initial job searching as well as in education, and the provision of services and facilities. It established the concept of genuine occupational qualifications, as well as positive action. Exceptions and special categories within the Act are complicated, and should be checked. The 1986 Act has been crucial to supporting changes in employment patterns of women, as many jobs are located in the lower-paid, part-time and lower-skilled areas of the national workforce. The Act is an important element in the establishment of women in their rightful place in the workforce. However, the statistics, particularly evident in the area of library and information work, indicate that women are not achieving economic or professional parity with men. It is, however, important to note that discrimination supporting women and discriminating against men is also unlawful. Positive action and positive discrimination are not the same – the former relates to practices which can help to achieve a more balanced workforce, and the latter is illegal. Sexual harassment is included in the Act through the application of 'less favourable treatment', but the Act is more difficult to enforce in this area. Further legislation may follow, but the 1986 Act considerably strengthened existing legislation.

Wages Act 1986
Includes conditions of employment, such as annual holidays, in industries covered by wages councils, and legislation concerned with wages payments within the scope of the Act.

Education Reform Act 1988
Major piece of legislation involving structural changes in education.

Includes a national curriculum, delegated financial responsibilities to Heads (Local Financial Management), changes in the status of the Polytechnics and their Governing Bodies. Established the PCFC and abolished the ILEA.

Employment Act 1988
This Act covers terms and conditions of employment, and the protection of individual workers, including contracts of employment, maternity pay and conditions, periods for giving notice, payment processes, national insurance contributions, unfair dismissal, redundancy payments, dismissal etc. Also concerned with recognition of trade unions, picketing, balloting and the implementation of codes of practice which would provide a balance for industrial relations in the eyes of the government. This includes a framework for union and employer consultations, as well as guidance on industrial tribunals procedures. The Act was fundamentally part of an initiative to support current political initiatives and so can also be seen in the context of changing political ideologies. The 1982 Act built on earlier legislation, and is particularly concerned with limiting the effect of the closed shop, and including compensation for workers dismissed for not being in a closed shop. Achieved through protecting and extending the individual rights of workers against restrictive union activities, and employers also able to restrain industrial action which is seen to support closed shop practices. Also established an independent commissioner for the rights of trade union members, to support individuals wishing to take action against their union in relation to the existing legislation. These Acts substantially amended the earlier Trade Union and Labour Regulations Act 1974, the Employment Protection Act 1975, and the Employment Protection (Consolidation) Act 1978. The latter also relates to the Sex Discrimination Act in that redundancy situations and retirement ages should not discriminate against women. All are complex.

Local Government Act 1988
Contains the important clause on the promotion of homosexual materials – particularly relevant to library and information services, and to selection policies.

Local Government Finance Act 1988
Abolished domestic rates and introduced the concept of the poll tax/community charge. Alternative scheme proposed as a result of legislation in March 1991.

Employment Bill 1989
Debated early in 1990. Continues the on-going debate on the closed shop. Illustrates radically changing political ideologies, as the GMB, for example, feels that the closed shop belongs to an earlier age. The Bill is seen by many on the left as in line with the European Commission's Social Charter, as it removes legal support for the pre-entry closed shop. Is similar in concept to the 1971 Industrial Relations Act. Clause 1 indicates the ethos of the Bill: *'Clause 1 provides that it is unlawful to refuse a person employment because he is or is not a trade union member, or because he will not agree to become or to cease to be a member, and that any person refused employment for such a reason may complain to an industrial tribunal.'*

Local Government and Housing Act 1989
Concerned with establishing parameters for the ways in which local authorities can use funds derived from the sale of assets, and the implementation of charges.

Note

Definitions
1 *Indirect discrimination.* Concerned with unjustifiable discrimination against a person of a particular sex or racial group. This involves the application of a condition or requirement which means that persons from the same sex or racial group who can comply with the condition is considerably smaller than other persons not of that group who are able to do so. Indirect discrimination takes place when a requirement or condition has the effect of discriminating unfairly between one group or individual and another.

2 *Direct discrimination.* Concerned with unjustifiable discrimination through the treatment of a person or group less favourably than other persons. The law is concerned that a person is not treated unfavourably on grounds of sex or race, and is not concerned with the motives of employers. Direct discrimination involves treating one person or group less favourably than another in the same circumstances.

3 *Racial grounds* are defined as: race, colour, nationality, ethnic or national origins. Racial group applies to a person within any of the above categories. Nationality includes the status of citizenship. Sexual discrimination applies to either sex (defined as male or female) or to marital status.

4 *Positive action* involves practices permitted under the legislation (Race Relations Act 1976 and Sex Discrimination Act 1975) which are concerned with redressing the effects of earlier discrimination. The legislation makes clear what practices are allowed and under what conditions, to give women and ethnic minority groups the chance to compete effectively in the areas of employment and education. (Exemptions to all Acts are detailed in the appropriate sections of the legislation.)

(Exemptions to all Acts are detailed in the appropriate sections of the legislation.)

Index

academic libraries, pay guide for 57
ACAS xiv, 155
accountability xii, xiii, 17, 117
administrative, professional, technical and clerical staff 25, 26
Advisory, Conciliation and Arbitration Service (ACAS) xiv, 155
ambition 114
ambivalence and change 47–8
anxiety
  change as cause of 45
  defence against 43–51
appraisal of staff 16–17
arbitration and conciliation 73
Association of University Teachers (AUT) 27, 59
AUT 27, 59

Battersea Park 97
behaviour of individuals 113
Benn, Melissa 119
black people *see* race
body language 32, 33, 35, 40–1
boycotting of library posts 56
British Association for Counselling 40
Buff book 25, 75
Burnham machinery 20, 27, 75

career scales 80
  see also grading levels
career structures in libraries 65–6

casualization 82, 83
Central Arbitration Committee 155
central government and libraries 69–70
change
  ambilance and 47–8
  as cause of anxiety 45
  in education 74–8
  in General Municipal Boilermakers (GMB) xv, 84–8
  in industrial relations 72–3
  managers and 111–14
  in organizations 45, 47–8, 111–14
  political aspects 116–21
Chartered Institute of Public Finance and Accountancy (CIPFA) 17
chief officers 36, 100, 101, 102, 104–5, 106, 118–19, 120
  see also local government, officers
child-care and TUC 7
CIPFA 17
Civil Service
  library pay guide 57
  secret report on employment in 82–3
clients
  idealization of 47
  service to 44, 50
closed shop xvi, 37
  legislation on 154, 155, 157, 159, 160
collective agreements 155

collective bargaining 37
colleges 60, 74-84
Combination Acts (1799; 1824; 1825; 1871; 1876; 1880) 153
commercial libraries, pay guide for 57
Commission on Industrial Relations 155
Commission for Racial Equality 4
community charge 91, 96, 97, 159
community groups 119
competitive contract tendering (CCT) 9, 14, 29, 97
conciliation and arbitration 73
conditions of work 24, 28, 29, 30, 33
  legislation 153, 155, 157, 158, 159
  in libraries 28, 60, 64-5
  college libraries 75-6, 79-80, 81-2
  see also negotiating machinery
conflict 47-8, 111-12, 114, 117, 118, 119
Conservative Government 71, 72, 73, 76, 80, 81-4 *passim*, 98
consumer choice 116-17
Continuing Professional Development (CPD) 111
core curriculum 74
counselling support 39-43
  defined 40
  referral in 41
  skills 40-1
covert behaviour 113
CPD 111
craft workers 25, 26
crisis management 119
cutbacks 63, 69, 70

de-skilling 45, 111
decentralization and devolution 116
decision making 117
defence mechanisms 43-51, 112, 114

demarcation 13
denial of the individual 45-6
depressive position 44, 49
development of women 11
devolution and decentralization 116
direct discrimination 4, 158, 160
direct labour force 97
Disabled Persons Employment Acts (1944; 1958) 153-4
discrimination 4, 158, 160
  see also equal opportunities; gender; race
disputes 73, 153, 154, 155, 157, 158, 159
division between 'professionals' and 'non-professionals' 46, 48, 65-6
dual labour market 8

education
  changes in xvii, 74-8
  GMB initiative on 88
  of managers 111
Education Reform Act (1988) xvii, 17, 18, 74, 76, 78, 91, 158-9
Education (Schools and Further Education) Regulations (1981+) 74
EEPTU xv
effectiveness, measurements of 19
efficiency, measurements of 18-19
Elected Members 100, 101, 103, 118
Electrical, Engineering and Plumbing Trades Union (EEPTU) xv
employees, information disclosure to 157
Employers Liability (Compulsory Insurance) Act (1969) 154
employers' organizations 25, 61
Employment Acts (1980; 1982; 1988) 157, 159
Employment Bill (1989) 160

employment law 152–61
Employment Protection Act (1975) 155, 159
Employment Protection (Consolidation) Act (1978) 156, 159
Environment, Department of 80
equal opportunities 4–5, 9, 57–8, 66–7, 87–8, 119
  legislation 154, 155, 156, 158, 159
Equal Opportunities Commission 4
Equal Pay Acts (1970; 1975) 154
ethnic minorities *see* race
Etzioni, A. 111

Federated Union of Managers and Professional Officers (FUMPO), links with Library Association 59
'female' occupations 8
feminine style of management 120–1
FEU 17
Financing our public library service (Green Paper) 17, 69, 70
flexi-time 82
flexibility
  employee-led 86–7
  employer-led 81–3
Ford of America xiv–xv
FUMPO, links with Library Association 59
Further Education Regulations (1975–7) 74–5
Further Education Unit (FEU) 17
Futures reports (1985) 55

gender 7–13, 13–14, 86, 87–8, 119
  issues in libraries 10–12, 66–7
  legislation on 4, 10, 153, 154, 156, 158, 159
  see also women
General Municipal Boilermakers (GMB)
  changes in xv, 84–8
  view on closed shop 160
GLES 25, 26
GMB
  changes in xv, 84–8
  view on closed shop 160
Goodall, D. L. 18
governors
  college 78, 79
  school 74
grading levels 67–8
  see also career scales
Gramsci, A. 121
Greater London Employers Secretariat (GLES) 25, 26
Green book 25, 101
grievances 33, 37
group behaviour 112–13, 114
group dynamics of workplaces xvii

Handy, C. 111
harmonization xvi, 13–15
  definitions of 13
  in libraries 15
Health and Safety at Work Act (1974) 155
health and safety at work legislation 154, 155
healthy organizations 106
HECs 76–7
Herzberg, F. 111
hidden agendas 33, 41
high profile libraries xvi, 70
Higher Education Corporations (HECs) 76–7
higher-education colleges *see* colleges; polytechnics
homosexual materials, promotion of 159
Hours of Employment Act (1936) 153
hybrid posts 75–6
hygiene factors 106

ILEA, abolition of 91, 93, 97
indirect discrimination 4, 158, 160

individualism 73
individuals
  behaviour of 113
  concern for 112
industrial relations
  legislation 71, 73, 154–5, 156, 157, 159, 160
  trends in 72–3
Industrial Relations Act (1971) 154–5, 160
Industrial Training Act (1964) 154
industrial tribunals
  and employer/employee relationships 30
  support for women 10
infants, defence mechanism of 43
information disclosure to employees 157
Institute of Professionals, Managers and Specialists (IPMS) 59

Jarratt Committee 17
job descriptions 29, 81
job evaluation 19, 29
joint local committees 25, 26–7
Joint National Committee for Chief Officers 25

Klein, Melanie 43–4, 113

Labour Party
  attack on local government officers 99–101
  conflict within 104
  draft policy document (1990) xvi
  and unions 103–4
language, negotiating 33, 35
learning 50
LEAs 76–9 *passim*
legislation
  education xvii, 17, 18, 74, 76, 78
  employment 152–61
  industrial relations 71, 73, 154–5, 156, 157, 159, 160
local government and housing xiii, xvi, 69
race relations 4
sex discrimination 4, 10, 153, 154, 156, 158, 159
LGMB 25
librarians
  pay 56–7, 60, 61, 64, 67
  see also 'professional' staff
library assistants
  career prospects 66
  pay 64
  see also 'non-professional' staff; pay, library staff
Library Association
  advisory and support services 58–9
  employee relations activities 56–7, 61–2
  and equal opportunities 57–8
  information role of 61
  initiative on polytechnic staff pay and conditions 60
  links with employers 61
  links with unions 59–60, 68
  publications 60, 62
  qualifications awards by 56
  role of 55–62
  Royal Charter objectives 55
  salary guides 56–7
  statements on personnel topics 57
  structure 61–2
  surveys by 59
  as a union? 60–1
  vacancies monitoring 56
  on violence in libraries 57
library staff
  see librarians; library assistants
Likert, R. 111
listening 35, 40
local accountability xii, xiii
local authorities *see* local government
Local Education Authorities (LEAs) 76–9 *passim*

local government
  attitudes to libraries 68–70
  departments 103
  officers,
    Labour Party attack on 99–101
    rewards and opportunities for 101–2
    see also Chief Officers
  reorganization 14
Local Government Act (1988) 159
Local Government Finance Act (1982; 1988) 157, 159
Local Government and Housing Act (1988) 69, 160
Local Government and Housing Act (1989) xiii, xvi
Local Government Management Board (LGMB) 25
local and national negotiation 77, 78, 79–81
London, local authority household projections 92

McGregor, D. 111
McKinsey framework for organizations 121
management
  attitudes to unions 44, 45
  conflict with unions 47–8
Management Charter Initiative 111
management circles 113
management context, changes in xi–xviii
management theory 111
management unions 36
management-information systems, staff involvement in 18
managers
  coping with change 111–14
  education and training of 111
  as facilitators 49–50
  and negotiation 30, 36
  and performance appraisal 22
  resource management role 50–1

roles of 112
skills of 113, 114
manual workers 25, 26
marginalization of minorities 5
market forces xii–xiii, 28, 29
Marris, P. 47
Maslow, A. H. 111
maternity pay legislation 155
Mayo, E. 111
meetings of workers, legislation on 153
Menzies, Isabel 43, 44, 45, 48
mistakes 48
monitoring
  for gender bias 10–11, 57–8
  for racism 3, 4, 7, 58
motivation 114

NALGO
  career structures 65–6
  hybrid posts 75–6
  left wing infiltration 118
  library pay and conditions 67–8
  links with Library Association 59–60, 68
  local and central government 68–70
  training and qualification 65
NATFHE
  Branches 79
  hybrid posts 75–6
  links with Library Association 59, 60
  role of 27
National Association of Teachers in Further and Higher Education see NATFHE
National Health Service, library pay guide 57
National Industrial Relations Court 154, 155
National Joint Councils 67, 75
national and local negotiation 77, 78, 79–81
negotiating language 33, 35
negotiating machinery 20, 24–31, 75, 76–81

negotiating machinery (cont.)
  see also conditions of work
negotiating process 26, 31–9
  agendas 33, 34
  defining outcomes 33
  groups involved 36–7
  micro-framework for negotiating 32–3
  pace and style 33–4
  tactics and strategy 37
  timing 34–5
negotiating skills 31–2, 35
negotiations, pay 27–8, 29, 33, 75, 76–81
new technology xvii–xviii
  and race 3–4
  and women 8
'no strike' deals xv
'non-professional' staff 46, 48, 65–6
  see also library assistants

OAL 17, 28
observing 35, 40–1
Office of Arts and Libraries (OAL) 17, 28
Offices, Shops and Railway Premises Act (1963) 154
opening hours 64
organizational change 45, 47–8, 111–14
organizational development 106, 113
organizations, size of 111
overt behaviour 113

paranoid/schizoid mechanisms 43, 44, 45–7
part-time staff 82, 85, 87, 88
pay
  college libraries 75–6, 78, 79–80, 81
  legislation 154, 155, 157, 158, 159
  library staff 56–7, 60, 61, 64, 66–7
  negotiations 27–8, 29, 33, 75, 76–81

PCFC 28, 76, 77, 79
performance appraisal 16–17
  personal relationships and 21–2
performance indicators 16–24
  for libraries 18–19
performance measurement, quantitative vs. qualitative 17
performance-related pay 16, 19–21, 28–9
personal relationships and performance appraisal 21–2
Peters, T. J. 121
play, value of 49–50
policy conflicts 117
political environment 89–90, 96, 116–21
political party infiltration 119
political relationships 105–6
politics and practitioners 98–107, 119–20
poll tax 91, 96, 97, 159
Pollitt, C. 17
polytechnics xvii, 37–8, 60, 77
Polytechnics and Colleges Funding Council (PCFC) 28, 76, 77, 79
Polytechnics and Colleges National Negotiating Committee 77
positive action 156, 161
positive discrimination 156
power 27, 35–6
pregnancy, protection against dismissal for 155, 156
presenting problems 27, 39
prioritization 117, 118
privatization 70, 71, 91, 94, 96, 97
  effect on women 9
procedural outcomes 33
production and extraction industries, decline of 72
'professional' staff 46, 48, 65–6
  see also librarians
professionalism 116, 117

Index

promotion 67
Provincial Councils 25, 75
psychodynamics 35, 38, 39, 43–52, 112, 114
public libraries pay guide 57
public support for libraries 69, 70
public-sector blueprint 82–3
Purple book 25, 75, 101

qualification in library service 65–6
 see also 'non-professional' staff; 'professional' staff

race 3–7, 9
 effect of new technology 3–4
 legislation on 4, 156, 160
 monitoring for racicm 3, 4, 7, 58
Race Relations Act (1976) 4, 156
recruitment
 and equal opportunity 4–5, 10–11
 monitoring for gender bias 10–11
 monitoring for racism 3, 4, 7
redundancies 96–7, 154
Redundancy Payments Act (1965) 154
referral in counselling 41
Registry of Trade Unions and Employers Associations 155
regrading of posts 59
Rehabilitation of Offenders Act (1975) 156
Richardson, E. 120
rotas 46
rules, disciplinary and grievance 37

salaries *see* pay
schools, changes in 74
service delivery 44, 50, 117, 118, 120
service industries, GMB recruitment in 87
service orientation 29

Sex Discrimination Acts (1975; Amendment 1986) 4, 156, 158
sex *see* gender
sexual harassment 9, 158
shared values 112, 118, 121
Silver book 27, 75
single unions xiv–xv, 13
single-status workforce *see* harmonization
social provision, decline in 72–3
splitting 45, 46, 48–9
staff
 caring for 11, 16
 development plan 106
 turnover 48, 119
staff appraisal *see* performance appraisal
staffing levels 64–5
standardization of conditions *see* harmonization
stereotyping of women 7, 10
stress, library staff 57, 65
strikes *see* disputes
substantive outcomes 33

targets, pay related to 20
Taylor, Robert 72
teachers, pay negotiation for 20, 27–8
teamwork, pay related to 20
tensions
 between local and central government xiii, 28–9, 116
 between professionals and politicians xii–xiii
 caused by change xi–xii
 in education xvii
 in workplaces xviii, 111–14
tiers of negotiations 25–6
time off for union activities 156
time wasting 13
Trade Disputes and Trade Unions Act (1948) 154
Trade Union Acts (1913; 1927; 1984) 153, 157–8

Trade Union and Labour
  Relations Acts (1974;
  1976) 155, 159
trade unions
  attitude to performance awards
    21
  attitudes to harmonization
    14–15
  attitudes to management 44,
    45, 118
  changes in xiv–xvi
  conflict with management
    47–8
  decline of 72, 85
  development in London 98–9
  disgruntled members of 72
  harmonization of see
    harmonization
  and Labour Party 103–4
  legislation on 153, 154, 155,
    156, 157–8, 159, 160
  local government officer
    involvement 101–2
  membership of ethnic groups
    3
  in negotiating process 36–7
  organization as balancing force
    xiii
  political initiatives 63
  single unions xiv–xv, 13
  structure 103
  women in 8–9
Trade Unions (Amalgamation)
  Act (1964) 154
Trades Disputes Act (1906) 153
Trades Union Congress see TUC
training
  GMB initiative on 88
  legislation 154, 155
  Library Association support
    for 57
  in library service 65
  managers 111
  for negotiating 38
  as play area 49
  women 11
Training Agency 77, 78
Training Enterprise and
  Education Directorate 78
transitional space 49–50
TUC
  changing role of xv–xvi
  and child-care 7
  Special Review Body xvi
  women in 9
tutor librarians 75–6

unfair dismissal, legislation on
  155, 156
unions see trade unions
unsocial hours 64

vacancies monitoring 56
values, shared 112, 118, 121
violence in libraries 57, 65
volunteers in welfare libraries
  57

Wages Act (1986) 158
Wages Councils Acts (1979) 157
Wandsworth, London Borough
  of 91–8
  consultation 93, 94
  future developments 95
  industrial relations 94, 96–7
  privatization 91, 94, 96, 97
  rating 91, 96, 97
  redundancies 96–7
  reorganization 93–4
Waterman, R. H. 121
'whole job', defining the 20
Winnicott, D. W. 43, 49, 50,
  113
women
  attitudes and aspirations 11
  discrimination against ethnic
    minorities 9
  legislation on employment of
    4, 10, 153, 154, 156, 158, 159
  in libraries 9, 10–11, 57–8,
    66–7
  management style 120–1
  motivation of 114
  pattern of work 7–8
  pay 66–7
  recruitment by GMB 86

women (cont.)
　in senior posts 8–9, 10, 11, 57–8, 67
　stereotyping of 7, 10
　training and development 11
　in unions 8–10
　see also equal opportunities; gender
work, attitude to 85
working conditions *see* conditions of work